THE MAGNIFICENT

7

Haynes Publishing

The enthusiasts' guide to every Lotus 7 and
Caterham 7 from 1957 to the present day

CHRIS REES

First published in 2002

A catalogue record for this book is available from the British Library

ISBN 1 85960 848 5

Library of Congress catalog card no 2001-135408

Published by Haynes Publishing, Sparkford, Yeovil, Somerset BA22 7JJ, UK

Tel: 01963 442030 Fax 01963 440001
Int. tel: +44 1963 442030 Fax +44 1963 440001
E-mail: sales@haynes-manuals.co.uk
Web site: www.haynes.co.uk

Haynes North America, Inc.,
861 Lawrence Drive, Newbury Park,
California 91320, USA

Printed and bound in England by J. H. Haynes & Co. Ltd,
Sparkford

Jurisdictions which have strict emission control laws may consider any modifications to a vehicle to be an infringement of those laws. You are advised to check with the appropriate body or authority whether your proposed modification complies fully with the law. The author and publishers accept no liability in this regard.

Contents

Acknowledgements

A great debt of thanks goes to Jez Coates at Caterham Cars, who spared much valuable time during a very busy period to talk about developments over the years, to share his incomparable experience with the 7 in terms of highlighting each model's strengths and weaknesses, and to read through and comment on the text of the book. I would also like to thank other people at Caterham who have offered invaluable help: Simon Nearn, Andy Noble, Jan Russell and Tony Murray, as well as James Whiting.

At LAT Photo Archives I would like to thank Tim Wright, at *Classic & Sports Car* magazine, James Elliott, Paul Hardiman and Mick Walsh, and at *Evo* magazine, Richard Neaden.

Introduction

Colin Chapman's first circuit racing car was the Lotus Mk 3. It laid down the template of light weight and minimalism that would later sire the 7, and became the car that established Chapman as a manufacturer of sports cars.

I have a strong and distinct memory from my childhood. At the age of about five, I was given a tiny book about four inches square, with fabulous painted illustrations of contemporary sports cars. Among the over-common MGs and overweight Astons, one car stood out. There was something about the poise of the car in the illustration – leaping out of the page front three-quarters on, cresting a rise, wheels off the ground, at full chat. The illustrator had caught the driver perfectly too: elbow jutting out of the side, body at an angle that betrayed sheer involvement, windswept clothing, and a look of pure contentment on his face.

Of course, that car was the Lotus 7 (I think they captioned the picture Lotus Super 7, which seemed very fitting to me). One thing was clear from that illustration and the table of figures next to it. There was no other car like the 7. A childhood mind may not have been impressed by the power output of the engine compared with the Ferraris which also populated the slim volume, or with its slender top speed (which I believe was the lowest in the whole book). But no other car was nearly as pure, as raw and – clearly from that illustration – half as much fun. As Graham Nearn of Caterham Cars later put it: 'Right from the start it was the ultimate sports car. It didn't seem worth bothering with anything else.'

I no longer have that childhood book, but the fact that I remember that picture above all others is testament to the emotional power of the Lotus

6

7. No two ways about it: the 7 is a car of passion. It inspires emotion, devotion, loyalty, but above all an appreciation of what makes it the purest essence of what a sports car is. Road testers exhaust superlatives, first-timers wear fixed grins that no words can fully convey, long-time owners share stories of great drives, great moments. Unlike other sports cars, there is no pretence to the 7; it is not exclusive, rarefied, flash or snobby, but accessible, honest and true to an ideal.

That ideal is down to one man, Colin Chapman. He famously said of the 7: 'It was simple and just kept going. The sort of thing you could dash off in a weekend. Well, a week maybe.'

By 1957, when he designed the 7, Chapman had already notched up some world-beating creations, including the Le Mans class-winning Eleven. The full story of the early years of Lotus is not something to tackle in this introduction, but we can trace the origins of the 7 in the earliest creations of the genius that was Colin Chapman.

In 1948, Chapman was an engineering student at London University, but he also dabbled in used car sales. When an old Austin 7 would not sell, he set about building the very first Lotus car, effectively a special, in a garage behind his girlfriend's north London home. A boxy marine ply sports body was all that was needed on top of the Austin chassis to go trialling. In 1949, Chapman moved on to British Aluminium, and his special building moved up a step with the Mark 2, a sports car based on an Austin 7 chassis with a Ford sidevalve engine.

It was the Mark 3 of 1951 (an all-alloy-bodied racer based on a modified Austin 7 chassis) that really drew the interest of other drivers, as members of the 750 Motor Club were attracted to Chapman's new circuit racer because it won so many events. Having built replicas, he was persuaded to set up Lotus Engineering as a part-time business on 1 January 1952, where he built the Mark 4 in 1954 for trialling.

The Lotus Mark 6 was an inspired road and race machine, the first Lotus to have its own purpose-designed chassis and the first Lotus to be manufactured in volume.

The Mark 5 never materialised but the Mark 6 would become easily the most important Lotus yet. Chapman created his first self-designed chassis based around two large rails, on to which was fabricated a lightweight spaceframe. The Progress Chassis Co. built the first Mark 6 chassis and coachbuilders Williams & Pritchard clothed it in a simple aluminium body with cycle wings, enclosed rear wings and a squarish nosecone. The template for the future 7 had already been set.

Basic Ford components were used for the Mark 6, which became the first Lotus to be sold in volume. A Ford 1,172cc sidevalve or linered-down 1,500cc Consul engine was fitted (occasionally an MG TC too), plus a divided Ford front axle and Ford 8 or 10 rear axle. Light weight

With the Mark 6, Lotus introduced the idea of the complete kit-form car. Simple aluminium body panels enveloped a steel tube space frame chassis.

was the key to the Mark 6's success; at just 8.5cwt (432kg), not much power was needed to make the car perform magnificently.

By 1953, the Mark 6 was in regular production, sold in kit form to escape the 25 per cent purchase tax levied on complete cars. Lotus was one of the first companies to produce kit cars but by offering bodies, chassis and most other specialist parts to complete a car, it was superior to other companies of the time. The engine, gearbox and axles (the latter modified by Lotus) would be sourced by the builder. Lotus quoted a typical on-the-road figure of around £400, which was excellent value.

The Mark 6 impressed everyone who drove it. *Autocar* achieved almost 90mph and enthused: 'There can be few, if any, cars which are quicker through sharp S-bends.' That's quite a statement considering how many excellent sports cars there were around at the time – and considering this was Lotus's very first production car.

As Chapman moved on to racing cars such as the Mark 8, 9 and 10, the Mark 7 slot was left open after the planned Mark 7 Formula 2 racer was left unfinished. Meanwhile, the Mark 6 was pushed to the back of Chapman's mind. As the Eleven began scoring significant victories and Lotus seemed set for the big time, the Mark 6 was taken out of production in late 1955 with around 110 cars built.

But there remained strong demand for a successor to the Mark 6. Chapman recognised that sales of racing cars were extremely seasonal, so for the sake of cash flow he set about a proper road car programme. First he created the all-glassfibre Lotus Fourteen (Elite), but this was a fiendishly difficult car to make and ultimately it would never be profitable. So it was that Chapman succumbed and almost literally threw together the 7 which was created at Chapman's home in Friern Barnet. Work began in spring 1957, with Progress Chassis building the prototype chassis and Williams & Pritchard constructing the first aluminium body. It would be ready for its first public outing in September 1957, but not actually entering production until the following year. Almost immediately, it became a legend among club racers.

Ironically, Chapman completely lost interest in the 7 almost as soon as he had created it. He was always moving on to the next step and had no desire to relive old glories. Yet for many years the 7 did provide the bread-and-butter income for Lotus to win its grands prix and remained a fixture at Lotus long past the time when Chapman would have liked to have seen it killed off.

The 7 emerged as the essential lightweight sports car. It was too pure for most drivers, who preferred to spend more money to get less out of the

It might have been a basic machine, but the Mark 6's combination of brilliant, no-frills engineering and simplicity gave it a dynamic edge that was hard for the enthusiast to ignore.

In a historic move, Colin Chapman (right) hands over the production rights for the 7 to Graham Nearn of Caterham Cars. The May 1973 ceremony cemented Caterham as the home of the 7 for the next generation.

equation in cars like the MG Midget. For a select band of owners, the Lotus 7 was the only car to own and moreover it was utterly accessible, virtually regardless of your budget.

The 7 progressed into a Series 2 in 1960, in which form it entered its longest period without alteration. The 7 virtually died in 1966 when Lotus switched premises, or would have done, had Graham Nearn of Caterham Cars not come up with an order for 20 cars which Lotus could not refuse to honour. Then came the Series 3 in 1968, bringing the 7 into the era of Ford crossflow and Lotus Twin Cam power. The Series 4 of 1970 was an aberration in the wider scheme of things, but entirely logical and actually quite a strong seller, despite the controversy of its greater bulk and quasi-beach buggy styling.

But by the early 1970s, the Lotus 7 sat uncomfortably in the Chapman master plan for Lotus. With the Elite and Esprit, Lotus would move decisively up-market and the 7 had no place in these plans. Fortunately, Graham Nearn of Caterham Cars, the longest-standing and most passionate Lotus 7 sales outlet, had already secured the 7's future. In 1971, Chapman had agreed to hand over the manufacturing rights of the 7 to Caterham, something that occurred in May 1973.

Caterham started by continuing Series 4 production, but it quickly became apparent that enthusiasts preferred the idea of a revived Series 3, which also happened to be much easier to make. So it was that in 1974, Caterham reverted to the classic 7 format – and has never looked back.

In the early days, 'development' as such was more like fire-fighting as various components – engines, rear axles, transmissions and so on – became unavailable. Gradually, Caterham shook itself out of a sort of slavery to the unaltering original design of Chapman's 7 and began applying its own engineering improvements. A longer cockpit, de Dion rear suspension and revised geometry all made their entrance in the early to mid-1980s. In due course it would develop its own six-speed gearbox and

It took until 1957 for the Lotus 7 to be launched, and it immediately became the essential lightweight sports car. Colin Chapman later declared the design had taken him just a week to complete.

Unlike many other performance cars, it is not a challenge to run a 7. Most of the engineering side is fairly straightforward.

produce its own engine specifications.

Caterham really got into the swing of things in the 1990s, developing the full potential of the 7 with a string of steadily more highly powered and lightweight cars. Cosworth BDR power gave way to the 175bhp Vauxhall HPC as new Caterham-originated legends were created. And no legend was more potent than the phenomenal JPE, essentially an ultra-lightweight 7 powered by a British Touring Car Vauxhall engine.

An engineering connection with Rover led to Caterham adopting the acclaimed K-series range of engines, which became the mainstay powerplant through the 1990s. These developed into a broad spread of options, from 103bhp right up to 230bhp in the most extreme Superlight R500 manifestation. Caterham even strayed from the rule that the 7's shape should always remain untouched, first with the elegant 21 and later with the longer, wider 7 SV. As for engines, the wheel is set to come full circle again in 2002 with the adoption of the Ford Duratec 2.0-litre engine, which will see the 7 return to its historical connection with Ford power.

It is a fact that not one single component on the latest Caterham 7 is shared with the Lotus 7 from which it has evolved. But the lineage is unbroken and absolutely clear, and no-one would argue that Caterham has been the most fastidious of 'custodians' of the legend that is the 7. It has constantly been fettled, improved, diversified but has never lost sight of the roots from which it has grown.

The 7 continues to pile up the accolades, regularly appearing in magazines' listings of the greatest cars of all time, consistently upsetting far more expensive and supposedly accomplished sports cars, and breaking records on test. One record that the 7 seems set never to lose is its status as the sports car that has remained in production for the longest time. Born in 1957, the 7 continues to this day as strong as it ever has been, approaching its 45th year in production. Well over 11,000 7s of all types have been built to date, qualifying it as the most successful kit-form car in history (eclipsing the Lotus Elan in second place).

If imitation is the sincerest form of flattery, the sheer number of lookalike 7s on the market pays the greatest compliment to the 7. Yet there is only one original, and that is Colin Chapman's 7, as produced by Lotus and Caterham. And as the saying goes, original is best. No-one has yet produced anything that approaches the engineering brilliance, the manufacturing quality, the peerless dynamic ability, or the enviable reputation that envelops the 7 right across the globe.

Simplicity is nearly always the key to long-lasting success, and the 7 keeps things just about as simple as you can get. There is no reason why the 7 should not continue in production indefinitely, remaining true to the ideals of light weight and the purest sports car responses.

This book aims to present the complete panoply of 7 derivatives, from the very first 100E-powered Series 1 Lotus to the latest motorbike-engined Caterhams. Even I was amazed to discover on totting them all up that there were no less than 54 major variations of the 7, plus numerous sub-variations. Each gets its own full description, with its place in the 7 universe charted, plus full coverage of its strengths and weaknesses, driving impressions, technical specifications, performance figures, production numbers and

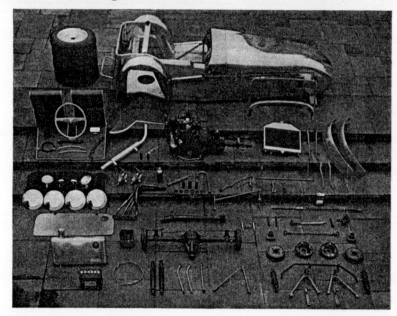

identification features. Copious illustrations provide, I hope, a visual feast and a full account of the 7 in all its forms.

It gives me enormous pleasure to have compiled a book which finally closes the loop on my childhood discovery of this superlative sports car. I now have something to rival the memory of the painting in that four-inch square book that inspired me to dream of the 7 all those years ago.

An early advert for the 7 extols the simplicity of the build process. From day one until the present time, the 7 has always been available in kit form as well as fully built.

Chris Rees
Berkshire, November 2001

Buying, running and restoring a 7

What sort of use do you want to put your 7 to? Will it be primarily for road use, for track day fun or for motorsport? This greatly affects the specification you should look for in a used car.

It is not everyone who can simply visit Caterham's excellent sales site in Caterham town centre and order a brand new 7 – which is what most of us would surely wish to do. Even if we could, there remains a waiting list for new cars, added to which most cars bought new are actually in kit or component form and you have to schedule in time to build the car too. Most potential 7 owners therefore do the next best thing – buy second-hand. And they have a huge choice indeed, for well over 10,000 7s of all types have been built to date. Something over 3,000 of those were original Lotus 7s but the vast majority of used cars out there today are Caterhams.

Unlike many used sports cars, a 7 can be both cheap and simple to run. It's not a complex car by any means; it lacks the sophisticated electronics, control systems, hinged panels and expensive trim of many potential rivals, for instance. It's also very well built from non-rusting aluminium and glassfibre, so a 7 can potentially live forever.

The 7 is extremely well supported not only by the factory but by a wide spread of dedicated specialists across the UK and elsewhere. Additionally, owners can benefit from the events, support and advice offered by the owners' club.

The down side of buying second-hand is that there are always fewer 7s than there are people who want to own one, so often a long search is necessary and purchase prices are often very high. But high demand does

mean that, when it comes to letting your 7 go, you will get back roughly what you paid for it; very slender depreciation is a powerful fringe benefit of owning a 7.

The variety of used models available is bewilderingly huge, as the pages in this guide reveal. At one extreme you may find a classic early Lotus Series 1 with an asthmatic Ford sidevalve engine. At the other you can brave getting behind the wheel of the death-defying Superlight R500, which in character and make-up has almost nothing in common with the early Lotus. That's not to say that, in their own ways, either car offers any less enjoyment – it's all a question of what you want from your 7.

Indeed, your very first question ought to be: what exactly do I want from a 7? Do you intend to use it as an everyday car for commuting? If so, are you aware of its limitations? Do you fancy a spot of competition activity? If so, in what sort of races? Do you want a car which you can work on (to restore or to modify, for example), or do you just want to get in and drive? Are you looking for performance and ultimate handling, or are you content to derive your pleasure from simply being in a 7? Perhaps most importantly of all, what is your budget?

Having raised all the questions, deciding exactly which model and specification you want may be a luxury you have to forego. While the population of 7s is increasing all the time, there is still a scarcity of used examples compared to most sports cars, and there is always very strong demand for good examples at the right price.

It's always a good idea to have in mind your ideal specification, but be prepared to compromise to get the right car. Many cars have been modified and there are almost as many varieties of 7 as there are cars built. As long as you have a basic idea of what you want from a 7 and are aware of the various types built, persistence will usually reap its own reward, even if you don't end up with precisely your ideal specification.

Most of us would like to be able to buy a 7 direct from the factory. Luckily, as well as new cars, the Caterham sales office in the centre of Caterham boasts a huge selection of pre-owned 7s at all different prices.

Lotus or Caterham?

Pubs have reverberated to the sound of 7 enthusiasts arguing over the comparative merits of Lotus and Caterham-built 7s, and no doubt will continue to do so. Die-hard enthusiasts often insist that the Lotus 7 is the true and original 7, and there is undoubtedly a mystique about the Lotus name. But in terms of dynamic ability and practicality the Caterham wins every time. Caterhams have stiffer chassis, better suspension, more direct steering, more powerful brakes, more modern engines and better weather equipment. The later you go the better the dynamics become. While the heart may cry Lotus, the head surely has to follow Caterham.

There is something uniquely alluring about an early Lotus 7, which explains the loyal and fanatical die-hard following they have. Series 1 and early Series 2 cars are especially sought after. But they are very hard to find and command very high prices. You're paying for mystique and rarity here, a heady mix of charisma and history. Most early cars are treasured possessions and it's very rare to find one for sale, so are really for the died-in-the-wool aficionado.

13

The Series 2 is the most common to find as it was produced for eight years. Most 'ordinary' 7s came with the Ford Anglia 105E engine but the Cosworth ones are the most sought after and most have been restored to this spec, with red interiors, green-and-yellow paintwork and Lotus wheels.

As for later Lotus 7s, Series 3 cars are relatively scarce and look very similar to the Caterham, which of course is a more practical proposition. The Twin Cam SS is undoubtedly the most highly regarded S3, but plenty of twin-cam engine transplants have been carried out, which brings us to the issue of originality. This is the absolute crux for all S1, S2 and S3 Lotus 7s, a pukka unmolested example being worth far more than a butchered-about one.

The Lotus 7 Series 4 is in many ways a special case. Its reputation as the poor relation of the 7 family will never go away. But low prices and Lotus badging make it appealing and it is dynamically no less fun to drive, and indeed,

Lotus or Caterham? While there is a view that the Lotus is the 'real' 7, the Caterhams are dynamically far superior, and of course more easily found on the used market. An aluminium Lotus 7 Series 1 and a Caterham 7 are posed at the redeveloped Caterham Cars sales site at the top of Caterham Hill in 1993.

probably the most practical Lotus 7 for everyday use. After Lotus finished with the 7, Caterham started building the S4 initially, but only 38 were made before it switched to the S3 from 1974.

The detail of what changes Caterham made to the 7 over the years is fully covered in the model-by-model section, but let's highlight the major changes that may affect your decision about which type to purchase. Early Caterhams used a modified version of the strengthened S3 Twin Cam SS chassis, providing superior handling characteristics. Most Caterhams in the 1970s were exported, and finding an early car is difficult. One thing is sure though: it will almost certainly have a Lotus Twin Cam engine fitted, and such cars will always be sought after. Lotus Twin Cam production effectively ended in 1981 with only just over 300 cars built.

From 1981, Caterhams came with a Morris Ital rear axle which is very robust and can handle large power outputs. Live axle cars have a tangible connection with the original Lotus and remain very popular even today. However, de Dion suspension, available on 7s from 1985, provides a much improved and more assured ride and the capability of handling more power. It is undoubtedly the superior set-up, and allows five-speed gearboxes to be fitted.

If you are a tall driver (6ft or over), it would be advisable to find a Long Cockpit Caterham (offered as a popular option from 1981 and standard

from 1992) – drivers up to 6ft 6in (2m) can fit in a Long Cockpit car, as long as they are not too wide. A further major advance was a five-speed gearbox option from 1986, giving better cruising ability. Rear disc brakes (1988), honeycomb side impact protection (1990) and Bilstein suspension (1991) were all significant advances which enhanced the appeal of the 7.

Perhaps the most important decision, and certainly the most perplexing, is which engine to choose. I have mentioned the Lotus Twin Cam engine as the classic 1970s powerplant, and it will always be in demand, although certainly not the most reliable or easy to keep in tune.

Without a doubt, the most common engine of all is the Ford Kent pushrod family. This was first fitted to 7s in 1968, was still available new in the mid-1990s and Caterham can still sell kits for second-hand Kent engines. In basic GT tune the engine has a mere 84bhp, which is quite sufficient for a bit of fun at weekends. More dedicated performance enthusiasts will prefer a Sprint or Supersprint version (between 100bhp and 135bhp). The latest entry-level 7s have switched to Vauxhall 1600 power and are every bit as good.

The Cosworth BDR-engined 7 is a rare and sought-after beast (therefore rather an expensive option), and in HPC guise is perhaps the most desirable of all 1980s 7s. If you want very high performance at reasonable cost the later Vauxhall-powered HPC is hard to beat, although the 7 did go faster in

Originality is the key with all Lotus 7s, especially early ones. This BMC-powered Series 1 is fairly easy to find parts for, but the Coventry-Climax engine is a real challenge.

Individual owners of course want to change their cars to suit their use, as with this Series 2, but the trend is definitely towards authenticity in Lotus 7s.

the ultra-rare JPE and recent Superlight R versions.

As for the Rover K-series engine, this has secured a reputation as one of the most fitting engines for a 7. It is now the most popular engine choice for component and fully built cars. As a second-hand choice numbers are constantly rising and they make a practical and rapid alternative to the more common Ford engine. Indeed, many regard K-series powered 7s as the sweetest of all. This applies even to the 1.4-litre version, although 1.6 and 1.8-litre engines are favoured in the marketplace. The VVC is a very strong all-round option.

The Superlight variants have a lot of kudos, and now represent the strongest selling Caterham as a new purchase. But be warned: these are by their nature extreme cars that are not suitable for daily use by and large. They are incredibly focused, and more fun than any other Caterham given an empty road and favourable conditions – ideally a circuit on a track day. Superlights are meant for driving when all you want to do is drive for the fun of it, not when you actually need to get from A to B. This is especially true of the Superlight R and R500 and even more so of the more recently launched motorbike-engined Blackbird and Fireblade.

General condition

The inherent value of a 7 generally means that cars are well looked after. As a result, it's rare to come across a 7 which is genuinely shabby; the days of neglected old wrecks are long gone. That said, the 7 has its weak points like any other car and condition does play an important part in pricing, but simply not as much as with other cars. One of the main reasons is that a 7 can be brought back to pristine condition fairly easily. The only exception would be a write-off where the chassis has been severely distorted.

A very important first step is to establish provenance. You need to be sure that the car is what the seller says it is. Check our Identification Features sections for individual models throughout this book to confirm the car's identity. Ask yourself if it has the correct engine. Ask about modifications, for many cars have been altered over the years. With earlier cars, originality pays dividends.

Perhaps most importantly, is the car you're looking at actually a 7? Lookalikes are extremely common and it is not unknown for sellers to pass them off as Caterhams. Most 'replicas' are actually nothing of the sort, usually suffering inferior quality, design deficiencies and major styling differences. Almost all alternative 7 types have less intrinsic value. So always take care to check the chassis and other identifying details against the registration document, which will also help you spot a stolen car. If in doubt, refer to Caterham for advice.

Next, ask if the car was factory-built, component-built or kit-built. This can make a difference to value, especially for later cars. Factory-built cars are obviously the most desirable: they have been specified as Caterham intended them, will have been constructed to the highest standard and have the strongest resale value.

The next stage is component built cars, i.e. sold in complete component form using all-new parts and requiring some level of build from the owner. All UK market pre-1984 cars were sold thus (basic kits first emerged in 1984) and this route remains a very popular option for new 7 buyers in Britain. All parts will have been new and the car is therefore likely to have a non-Q registration, which is preferable. The car will probably have originally been built to Caterham's standard – ask if the original builder took up Caterham's post-build inspection service.

From 1984, Caterhams have been available for sale in basic kit form. This is the cheapest option for new car builders, with parts supplied in packages. Most kit-built cars are likely to have some element of second-hand parts, such as the engine, gearbox or rear axle. Cars originally built with more than one major component that is second-hand cannot be registered as 'new' in Britain and therefore will carry a 'Q' registration prefix. There is some stigma attached to a 'Q' plate, partly because it identifies the car as being built from used parts, but also because you are stuck with a 'Q' plate – the DVLA will not allow you to swap registration plates to a non-Q.

Inevitably, more care needs to be taken when looking at a kit-built 7. You will need to satisfy yourself that the car was properly screwed together in the first place. Did Caterham check the car after build? Also bear in mind that the story behind any second-hand parts fitted is rarely clear. Expect to spend money recommissioning what were almost certainly used engines, gearboxes and axles when originally fitted.

Chassis

There is so little to a 7 that you could almost say a 7 *is* its chassis. Therefore chassis condition must come at the top of the list of checks. Although replacement chassis and repair sections are available for all 7 types, it takes high levels of skill to do it – it's definitely best left to the professionals. Arch Motors (Lotus and Caterham 7 chassis builders for around 30 years) can repair any chassis to 'as new' condition quickly and cost effectively. Replacing an entire chassis can, in some cases, also be viable (the cost is typically up to £5,000).

Originality is essential in a Lotus 7 especially. Lotus painted its chassis duck-egg blue on the S1 early S2, dark grey on other S2 and most S3s and

You can almost say a 7 *is* its chassis, so the condition of this is absolutely vital. This de Dion Supersprint chassis shows just how simple the whole affair is, but you need to check for bent and repaired tubing, while rust can seep from the inside out.

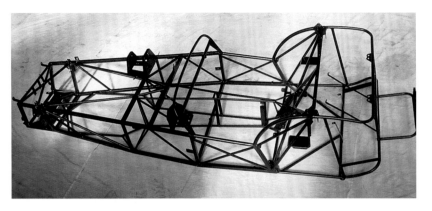

If your 7 has accident damage, replacement sections are readily available from the original manufacturer, Arch Motors. The usual replacement is the front end, available in both long and short sections.

black on late S3s. The triangulations changed with the S2 and Caterham strengthened the chassis when it relaunched the S3.

Check List
Accident damage – Signs of accident damage are your major concern. Luckily, most areas of the 7's chassis are easily visible and provide excellent clues about what sort of life the car has led. Well over half of accidents are frontal impacts, so particular attention should be paid to the engine bay area. First and particularly second suspension legs are the most likely areas to be damaged in any impact involving a front corner. The chassis tubes should be straight and have no joins in them, except at the nodes.

Chassis sections are available from the factory to replace front end damaged parts. Both 'short front' (first 12 inches of the chassis with all the front suspension pick-ups, ending immediately behind the second suspension leg), or the 'long front'(which extends back to the rear of the pedal box) are available. Both sections – if fitted correctly – can constitute a good-as-new repair. The only give-away is the disturbance to the protective powder coating finish which will be burnt away where the brazed joints are made. Air drying paint is usually sprayed over these areas on factory repairs, which is inevitably less durable. Look out for sprayed repairs as a sign of a pukka factory repair. Always ask about signs of repair and who undertook the repair (documented evidence should be available).

Checks should also include all areas of the chassis for bent tubes and breaking joints. To look for evidence of repair work, take off the bonnet and nose cone. Also check for a creased undertray. Drive the car and 'feel' if there is misalignment from a previous repair. Be aware of the car pulling to one side and bad creaking under acceleration, while you should be suspicious of uneven tyre wear.

Rust – This is not a major problem. However rust can begin inside the chassis tubes and then work its way outwards, making detection difficult. Check the tubes surrounding the suspension pick-up points front and rear and the lower side tubes which are crucial to rigidity. Suspension stress can cause fatigue on mounting points, while the vertical tubes where the rear radius arms mount to the chassis can distort. Jacking damage is also common. Any extra riveted panels on the aluminium bodywork should raise alarm bells – they might be concealing rust.

The Lotus S4 is a special case. The very different chassis/body design does harbour water and mud, resulting in plenty of scope for rust to take hold in the spaceframe. The fact that the glassfibre bodywork 'hangs' over the steel chassis makes matters worse, as serious repairs require the removal of bonded panels, an expensive process. Look at the tray where the steering and suspension are mounted; if there's rust here it's a fair bet that you'll find it elsewhere too.

Stressed aluminium panels – Aluminium to all intents and purposes does not corrode, which is a big advantage. However it does damage easily, so look at the floorpan and around the transmission tunnel for ripples, cracks, dents, tears and loose panels. Repairs can be expensive because work on stressed panelling should really be left to the professionals.

Bodywork

Unlike almost every other car, the condition of the bodywork has very little significance for a 7, at least as far Caterhams are concerned. Indeed, the bodywork is only critical on early all-aluminium bodied Lotus cars, where originality takes precedence. The cost of recreating the aluminium wings and nose cone can also be prohibitive.

For other 7s the good news is that the bodywork is very easy to recommission if it's damaged. Neither the aluminium panels nor the glassfibre rusts, although exterior aluminium panels can dent easily. If the main bodywork is unpainted – as on many cars it is – it needs careful wiping down after exposure to salt. Failure to do this can result in pitting. Polishing the aluminium regularly also helps maintain its good condition.

The glassfibre nose and wings on 7s are susceptible to accident damage and stone chipping but, on all 7s except the Lotus S4, they are detachable in next to no time and very cheap to replace. All standard colours are usually kept in stock among Caterham agents. The Series 4 is a different story; its method of construction (incorporating integral rear wings, scuttle and dashboard) means that body-off repairs are very involved. The front section is more easily removable. The self-pigmented S4 bodywork is prone to colour fade and most by now have been repainted conventionally, so look carefully at the quality of the work. All repairs must have been done properly to avoid paint stress cracks and blisters appearing.

Carbon fibre has become an increasingly popular material for the Caterham 7. Introduced on the JPE and popularised on the Superlight, carbon fibre wings, nose cone, wing protectors and interiors are de rigueur for many 7 owners, so much so that in 2001 Caterham began offering a carbon pack on its options list.

Bodywork is hardly an issue on a 7, as all the glassfibre panels are easily replaced. However, the condition of the stressed aluminium body panels is more critical, as they are easily dented, torn and creased.

On Caterhams, it is not viable to swap cycle wings for flared wings or vice versa. The holes for fitting the flared arches are drilled into the side panels, and these aluminium panels themselves must be changed. All wide-track suspension 7s must have cycle wings. Ironically, flared wings – having replaced cycle wings in 1960 – are now very much out of fashion. Cycle wings having been reintroduced for legislative reasons for the German market in the 1980s, the factory now reports that no-one orders flared wings any more and has deleted them from its latest catalogue.

Engines

Before examining each engine's strengths and weaknesses individually, some general points about 7s. Whatever engine is fitted, engine mounts should be checked, for new mounts can indicate crash damage. The condition of the low-slung sump can also reveal much about how the car has been treated. Most owners will have fitted stainless steel exhaust systems, which are therefore very long-lasting. For Caterhams equipped with catalysts, a non-catalysed competition exhaust system is a common retro-fit.

Lotus 7 engines – A wide variety of engines was fitted to the Lotus 7. While originality counts for virtually everything as far as Lotus 7s are concerned, it is a rare car indeed that retains its original powerplant. This is especially true of sidevalve and BMC A-series powered cars, whose humble motors are viewed as being a waste of the chassis. The best advice is not to be too concerned about engines – anything unsuitable can be replaced relatively easily with a more authentically correct powerplant.

But you need to exercise care with rarer and more valuable engines. The most precious S1 engine is the Coventry Climax, a delectable rarity fitted to the very first Super 7. But be warned: rebuilding this engine can cost almost as much as the rest of the car put together, and the engine itself is prone to internal corrosion and cracked cylinder heads.

For the S2, the dream engine to find would be the 1340 Cosworth, but again this is a very rare item and it does not have the best reputation for reliability, as its three-bearing bottom end will not stand high revs. A 1500 Cosworth engine is a good second best, while many S2s have non-Cosworth Cortina 1500 engines.

The S3 came with pushrod power (described below) or rarely with the Twin Cam engine (many have been fitted retrospectively). The S4 often came with Twin Cam power from the factory.

Twin Cam – Initially the Twin Cam engines in Caterhams were genuine Lotus units but from the late 1970s these were constructed by Vegantune and quality was variable. Later Caterham units used a Ford 1600 block, taking capacity up from 1,558cc to 1,598cc.

All Twin Cam engines need looking after. If they are properly serviced, they can be reliable and consistent. Once neglected, power and performance can drop significantly and the cost of overhauling a Twin Cam is much higher than any of the pushrod Ford units.

For example, changing the troublesome water pump requires removing the cylinder head, while the camshaft drive chain and tensioner wear quickly and, because of the seal-less valve guides, oil consumption tends to be high. On the parts side, the only problem with the Twin Cam is an acute shortage of cylinder heads.

Ford pushrod – The main advantage of Ford power is that the Kent engine is practical and reliable, with plenty of spares back-up (although some parts are now becoming scarce) and masses of tuning potential. Although the engines have to haul less weight around, they tend to get much harder use in a 7 than the Escort or Cortina they were designed for. Listen for piston slap and watch for blue exhaust smoke. Also be sure that any tuning that has been carried out has been done professionally. The more highly tuned the engine, the more hassle it will give. Race-spec engines might sound attractive in an advert but the pain of actually running something as temperamental as a full race engine will far outweigh the pleasure it gives when it's on song.

If you want a more powerful Ford engine the best course of action is to find a 7 Sprint or, even better, a Supersprint. These Caterham-modified engines are reliable and widely known. The Sprint unit, introduced in 1980, is a mild reworking of the Ford Kent 1600 engine, tuned to produce 110bhp (later 100bhp). The Supersprint unit, available from 1984, is bored out to 1.7 litres and has more goodies (larger valves, fully worked head, Kent cam and twin Webers). Producing 135bhp, it is probably the most practical way to reach the upper echelons of what the 7 can achieve. It's also the most commonly fitted engine among cars built by the factory. Your only real concern is that Weber carbs are notorious for being awkward to keep in tune.

Ford engines show their age in the sense that they do need regular decokes and do not last nearly as long as modern engines before needing a rebuild, which can cost anything up to £1,000.

Working on the engine is very simple because of the generous space around it. Ford crossflow parts are no problem whatsoever, but those for Twin Cam units can be more awkward to source.

Cosworth BDR – Although based on the Ford crossflow block, the tuned Cosworth engines are more temperamental because of their higher tolerances. In 1600 form, the engine develops 150bhp; in 1700 guise, the output is 170bhp. Weeping head gaskets were a common problem even when the units were new. Constant adjustment is needed to keep these highly tuned engines in the peak of performance. But there is no denying that a Cosworth engined 7 – particularly the rare HPC – is one of the most desirable of all, and prices reflect this.

Vauxhall HPC – The Vauxhall 2.0-litre engine which superseded the Cosworth as the standard HPC engine in 1990, is undoubtedly one of the most reliable of the high-powered engines fitted to a 7. Its 175bhp (or 165bhp in fuel-injection form) is extracted from a virtually standard Vauxhall powerplant (it's the same power unit fitted to the Calibra). Reliability, spares and servicing are not a problem, although carb-equipped engines need some leaded fuel – about one in every five fill-ups.

The engine is heavier than other units so it may be that it has caused stress in other areas such as the suspension or steering. Check especially for the integrity of the engine mounts and the exhaust system. Many Vauxhall engines have been tuned because of the ease with which extra power can be extracted, usually via 'superchips'. As Caterham proved with its Evolution upgrades and of course the JPE, figures of 210bhp to 250bhp can be attained without recourse to turbocharging. Always ask about any mods done to the engine, as the quality of some tuning packages is questionable.

The 1700 Supersprint engine is known to be reliable for a tuned unit, but its twin Weber carbs need constant adjustment to keep them in tune at the 135bhp it should develop.

Vauxhall 1600/1800 – Caterham switched to Vauxhall 1600 power in 1997, after Ford Kent blocks had ceased production. A virtually all-square twin-carb unit, it is very common, having been fitted to countless Astras and Cavaliers. There are no major servicing problems to deal with, but a tired engine will reveal itself by blue smoke from the exhaust, oil leaks and ticking camshafts. Caterham offered its own bored-out 1.8-litre Supersprint version.

Rover K-series – Perhaps the most practical and reliable of all engines fitted to the 7 is the Rover K-series engine, launched in 1991. Many hundreds of cars have now been fitted with this power unit and used examples are increasingly common. The K-series is a standard Rover engine (the 1.4 was fitted to the Metro GTi) and can even be serviced by Rover dealers thanks to an agreement between Caterham and Rover. There are unlikely to be any serious problems with any K-series engine, which has expanded to include 1.4, 1.6, 1.8 and 1.8 VVC types.

Pre-1993 engines will almost certainly be non-catalysed. Later engines may well be catalysed, identified by a rear-exiting exhaust or side-mount exhaust with an extended heat shield. The catalyst is large and made of a high-tech metal substrate, so power loss is minimal; but beware of damaged units, as replacement can be costly. The soundness of cats is now part of the MoT test. Also check that the foam pad that prevents oil surges has been replaced annually.

The K-series Supersport engines, (tweaked to produce 128bhp in 1.4-litre guise, 133bhp in 1.6-litre and 140bhp in 1.8-litre) were jointly developed by Rover and Caterham. These have become very popular, at one stage being fitted to 75 per cent of all K-series 7s. The Supersport option has been around since 1993 and seems to share the strengths of the standard K-series unit – certainly the unit has been successfully raced without reliability problems. The maintenance of this Caterham-branded engine should be entrusted to Caterham-approved sources.

Likewise, the more highly tuned VHPD K-series engine was another Caterham/Rover joint project. This 190bhp engine is an absolute gem but with more than 100bhp per litre it requires meticulous servicing and needs to be kept in tip-top condition to return its full compliment of power. The 230bhp Superlight R500 version of the 1.8 K-series is a highly specialised engine which should always be looked after by a Caterham-approved agent.

Honda Superbike – In 2000, Caterham officially engineered a 7 for Honda Blackbird power. This remains an extremely rare beast but a corollary of its high performance is that its longevity is impaired. Bike engines are doing well if they go much beyond 40,000 miles and the Blackbird engine is a very expensive one to replace. Bear in mind that the Caterham is a much heavier machine than the bike the engine was designed to power, so it does put stress on the engine.

The issue is perhaps more pertinent with the more recent Fireblade, as most owners fitted second-hand engines to keep costs down. While the supply of these is much better – the FireBlade engine has been in production since 1992 – fitting a replacement engine because the last one is worn out is not what you want to be doing.

Non-standard engines – Generally speaking, don't be tempted by a 7 fitted with a non-standard engine. Caterham does not recommend alternative engine choices and will not service non-sanctioned engines. There are examples of 7s running with all kinds of units from Alfa Romeo to Toyota twin cam, Mazda rotary to Ford CVH, Ford Zetec to Rover V8, but the used value of a car so fitted reflects what most people think of them. The weight difference of alternative engines can upset the handling balance and can even affect safety. If you are tempted by the cheap asking price of a non-standard 7, make doubly sure of the soundness of areas like engine mounting points, suspension set-up, ignition, exhaust systems, plus extra stresses on the chassis and on the rear axle.

Suspension

The rear axle on Lotus 7s is perhaps its greatest weakness. It started out with a Nash Metropolitan live axle, now rare, and switched to the Standard Companion axle with the Series 2 in 1960. The Companion axle does leak and eventually breaks if stressed too greatly, so it will often have been replaced with something more robust (Ford Escort or Morris Marina). Also the A-frame on post-S1 cars subjected excessive stress to the axle casing.

On Caterhams, the rear axle has changed over the years. The original Ford Escort axle switched to an Escort RS in 1977 but most common will be the Morris Marina/Ital rear axle used from 1981; equally likely is a Sierra-based de Dion rear end (optional from 1985 and now standard on all new cars).

Check for oil leaks from the diff and drums on the Ital axle. Also, if the car has a powerful engine fitted (above 150bhp), you should be aware that standard live axles are not ideal; the insides can't really cope with this sort of power. Again look for oil leaks as a sign of axle distortion. Reconditioned rear axles (both Ford and Ital) are quite easy to find – indeed, Caterham still builds some of its basic models with reconditioned Ital axles. On live-axle cars remember that many units were reconditioned in the first place and may now be very old.

The de Dion rear end has proven almost unburstable in use and can

Wheel bearings need to be checked on all four corners. The front suspension is very accessible, but most of your checks should concentrate on the rear end.

handle very much higher power outputs than either of the live axles. The rubber bushes in the rear A-frame are very hard worked and can start to knock out after only a few thousand miles. These need to be replaced regularly (handling suffers with wear) but thankfully the exercise is cheap and simple (post-1994 cars used a more robust bush that effectively eliminates this problem). Wheel bearings all round tend to get a pounding and this can affect handling. The front suspension is very easy to inspect and can be used as a good gauge of how well the car has been looked after generally.

Gearbox

The proprietary gearboxes used for most 7s are generally very robust and cheap. The S1's three-speed Ford or four-speed BMC gearbox are well catered for. A common problem on S2/S3 Cortina or Classic 'boxes is a tendency for vibration to shear the gearbox mountings.

On early Caterhams (1974-80), the gearbox is the Ford Corsair 2821E four-speed unit but far more common is the Ford Escort Sport Mk 2 unit that took over in 1980. The option of a close-ratio Sierra XR4-type five-speed box first became available in 1986 and has proven a popular choice. All units suit the various Ford engines, the HPC should have five speeds, while the K-series is best suited to Caterham's own six-speed unit (though the 1.8 is actually suited to the five-speed better).

Apart from the usual minor oil leaks, the off-the-shelf Ford 'boxes are very reliable and, in the event of malfunction, cheap to repair and replace. The only exception is with the K-series and Vauxhall-powered HPC models, both of which have their own special bell housings in aluminium, but the gearboxes themselves are standard (the Vauxhall engine requires that 10mm be cut at the input shaft). Clutches can suffer under the heavy use associated with driving a 7 but again replacement is not expensive.

Caterham's own six-speed gearbox, first produced in series in 1995, did suffer teething problems in the early days but these were resolved by 1996. Since most of the insides are derived from Ford parts, it is actually a fairly robust unit. However if there is a major problem, replacement is very expensive at around the £2,500 mark.

Brakes

Being so lightweight, the 7 puts very little stress on braking components and both pads and discs last much longer than most normal cars. Even on Lotus models, there are no real parts or service issues. Cars with live rear axles can only have rear drums (Ford or Morris). De Dion-equipped cars almost always come with four-wheel discs, which is naturally preferable (between 1985 and 1988 9-inch Sierra drums were standard). A huge variety of brake systems has been fitted to 7s, from standard components right up to full race spec items. Make sure your specification suits the use to which you will be putting the 7.

Interior

The state of the interior is only really an issue with the Lotus 7, for which originality counts for so much. And originality is rare, for most cars have been 'updated', many were stripped for racing and seats, steering wheels and instruments have often been replaced.

Correct Smiths dials and AC minor dials are favoured, as is the wood-rim steering wheel fitted to most S2s (the S1 Wilmot Breedon white plastic wheel is ultra-rare but looks unsuitable in the 7). Likewise the original Lotus wheel fitted to the S3 is another rare find.

Interiors are often tatty because of frequent exposure to the elements. On Caterhams, cloth seats fade so vinyl or leather is preferable (half leather or full leather interiors were expensive options but their day has well and truly passed and popularity has waned dramatically). Composite and kevlar seats are found on high-spec modern lightweights. Don't worry about carpets as these are cheap to replace.

By far the most desirable gearbox is the Caterham six-speed unit, which is based on Ford internals and therefore durable in use. Ford four and five-speed boxes are more common.

Weather equipment

Hoods on 7s are very simple in design. They are all held in place by popper fasteners and do deteriorate with use. Faded Perspex screens, hood shrinkage, tears, leaks and missing fasteners are all common and they can be fiddly to erect. If not folded correctly, they are prone to damage, and you should always check condition before deciding whether to buy. However soft-tops are well made and the cost of replacement is low compared with most soft-top sports cars.

The improved visibility weather protection introduced in 1988 is much more practical than the earlier type, in particular providing better elbow room, better visibility and the opportunity to stow the sidescreens in the boot. However, the rigid folding sidescreens cannot be fitted to the original-type hood; if you want to upgrade, you must change the whole hood.

The condition of the interior depends on its exposure to the elements, but it is tough and easily recommissioned. High-spec interiors such as this full-leather example need more care.

History

Knowing the history and background of your 7 is very important. A factory-built car has more kudos than a kit-built one for example, because of the guaranteed nature of its original build. However, Caterham has only recently started to issue service books with new cars.

Who has been looking after the 7? Is it an enthusiastic, knowledgeable owner or a hit-and-hope novice? Is it a specialist in 7s or the local garage? Specialised care and attention is very valuable with a 7 and a car with a proven record of having been looked after is far more desirable, value-enhancing and all round a better bet.

A 7 should be serviced every year at least once, whether it has been thrashed around race circuits or kept up on its axles. With cars that go on the track, a slightly overfilled oil reservoir is a good sign because it shows the owner knows about keeping lubrication going during hard cornering. Regular oil changes are also vital.

Originality adds value to a 7 – the Lotus more so, but increasingly with Caterhams too. With a Caterham it's a simple matter to check with the factory – which has records of all cars against their chassis number – to see what the original spec was. Cars are often known within the owners' clubs too.

It is a fact that 7s tend to be modified to suit individual owners' tastes. From simple things like changing the wheel and tyre choice up to major changes to suit serious track use, you need to be sure that the modifications are sound, safe and of good provenance. Modifications can enhance a car's value but they need to come documented from a respected source – preferably a Caterham-approved agent.

With a new dedicated aftersales department, you can entrust the servicing and modification of your 7 to the factory at Dartford.

7F Series 1

The original lightweight sports car

The very first Lotus 7 was the Ford sidevalve-powered Series 1, launched in 1957. Simple yet brilliantly engineered, it founded a dynasty that survives and thrives to this day.

With the Lotus 6, Colin Chapman had created a car that could not only win races convincingly, but a sports car that many average enthusiasts could afford to own. The fact that it had ended production in 1955 with no successor left many such enthusiasts crying out for something similar.

Latent demand for a successor and (perhaps more significantly for Lotus) a need for cashflow to support the official team racing campaigns led Colin Chapman to put together the 7 almost in his spare time – 'the sort of thing you could dash off in a weekend', said ACBC. The result was to become a legend that today looks set to continue well past its 50th birthday.

The new Lotus 7 was actually launched publicly in October 1957, virtually contemporaneously with the Elite, or Mark 14; the number 7 had been left blank for a Formula 2 project for the Clairmonte brothers that was never completed by Lotus. In fact, it would be many months before production actually began (Spring 1958 being the date that

The humble Ford 100E sidevalve engine was not the most exotic unit available, but it fitted the 7's role as a cheap-to-buy no-nonsense sports car. With twin carbs, the engine developed only 48bhp.

26

the first cars came into owners' hands).

The 7's chassis was a simple but brilliant affair, taking inspiration from both the 6 and the 11, the latter inspiring the design of the centre section, tunnel, axle mounts and scuttle. One-inch main tubes were supplemented by ³/₄in secondary tubes and the aluminium floor and transmission tunnel formed an integral part of the stressed structure, much like the 6. The Series 1 was unique among Lotus 7s in having all-aluminium bodywork, including the nose cone and wings which would in subsequent series be made of glassfibre. The early 7 also had a rear undertray which was not on later versions.

While the prototype Series 1 car, first seen in September 1957, had a Lotus 11-inspired de Dion rear axle, four-wheel disc brakes and a Coventry Climax 1,100cc engine, costs dictated that such an exotic specification needed to be cooled down; after all, this was meant to be a budget car for the impecunious enthusiast. Therefore the Lotus 11 de Dion rear end was swapped for the 11 'Club' version, consisting of a contemporary Nash/Austin Metropolitan live rear axle located by twin trailing arms and a single link from the offside end to the rear of the transmission tunnel. The front suspension was as per the Lotus 12, in other words lower wishbones, an anti-roll bar and upper links that formed the upper wishbones. As for the final drive unit, the standard Metropolitan 4.875:1 axle ratio could be adapted according to use, either shorter at 5.375:1 or longer at 3.730:1.

Another part of the paring down exercise from the prototype 7 was to abandon the expensive four-wheel discs in favour of Ford-sourced drums all round. These were activated hydraulically, with twin leading-shoe cast-iron drums of 8in diameter both front and rear. As for the choice of wheel, most Series 1 cars had 15 x 4-inch lightweight steel rims fitted with 520 x 15-inch crossply tyres. Initially these were made by Rubery Owen but some cars from 1960 had Triumph TR3 wheels.

Very early cars (thought to be the first 25 produced) had a Burman worm-and-nut steering box fitted, but this was soon changed to a modified Morris Minor rack-and-pinion unit. In both cases, it was mounted behind the front axle line. From October 1959, the first Triumph Herald racks were used in the Series 1.

Of all the specification changes in the production version, the most important of all was to defer the Climax engine installation (it would have to wait until the later Super 7). Instead, the first Series 1 cars would rely on the trusty Ford 100E sidevalve unit, substituted for a variety of reasons. First, it was cheap of course, and also very plentiful and widely used at the time in sports cars and specials. Additionally, it was ideal for racing in the 750 Motor Club's 1172 Formula.

The key to the success of the 7 was the way that it handled. Other cars may have been faster in a straight line – the Ford engine was hardly the most powerful powerplant – but virtually nothing could beat a 7 around a good bend.

Specification	
Engine	Ford 100E sidevalve
Capacity	1,172cc
Bore x stroke	63.5 x 92.5mm
Induction	Single Solex or Zenith carburettor (optionally twin SU)
Compression ratio	7.0:1 (optionally 8.5:1)
Max power	28–40bhp (21–30kW) at 4,500rpm (optionally 48bhp (36kW))
Max torque	52lb ft (70Nm) at 2,500rpm (optionally 58lb ft (78Nm) at 2,600rpm)
Gearbox	Ford three-speed
Brakes	8in drums front and rear
Steering	Modified Morris Minor rack-and-pinion (very early cars Burman worm-and-nut, later cars Triumph Herald)
Weight	918lb (416kg)
Top speed	78mph (125.5kph)(with optional engine 81mph/130kph)
0-60mph	19.0sec (with optional engine 17.8sec)
50-70mph in top	N/A (with optional engine 16.5sec)
Number produced	242 (all Series 1)

In standard tune, the 100E engine developed a meagre 40bhp. This was hardly the stuff of dreams by modern standards and only one other standard 7 engine (the BMC A-Series) developed less power. Yet performance was still lively by the standards of the day because the 7 weighed so little; Colin Chapman's ideal of slender weight was in full flow, and the 7 weighed under 1,000lb.

Stark, purposeful and unpretentious; the very early Lotus 7 established the founding principles abided by the 7 from the outset until the current day.

An extra 8bhp was available by fitting a Lotus-supplied tuning kit consisting of twin SU carburettors, a four-branch exhaust, stronger valve springs, polished ports, worked cylinder head and a higher compression ratio, all for £31 4s. The standard gearbox was Ford's archaic three-speed manual unit, although close-ratio gears were optional at £16 10s.

The cabin was utterly basic. A speedometer sat in front of the driver, with an oil pressure gauge and water temperature gauge sited either side of it, while an ammeter was slung out on the passenger side. There was no standard rev counter, or even a fuel gauge. The quickly detachable windscreen had no standard wipers, but a top-mounted wiper and motor could be fitted. As for lighting, one headlamp would extinguish on dipped beam, the brake and rear lights were combined and there were no indicators at all. A hood and tonneau were strictly optional.

The press at the time was highly enthusiastic, *Autocar* highlighting its 'exhilarating performance' and 'general stability' and concluded that it was the 'ideal road and race car.' Despite the archaic nature of many of the components, even today a sidevalve-powered Series 1 offers a surprisingly high degree of fun to drive. It was not a quick car by modern standards, and the strange gearing of the three-speed 'box meant that 37mph was possible in first gear.

Edward Lewis piloted the prototype 7 at the Brighton Speed Trials in September 1957 – the very first time the new car had been seen in public. It had disc brakes and a de Dion rear axle, unlike production 7s.

But overall the feeling of being at one with the machine is possibly greater in this earliest of 7s than any other. Its handling is instinctively right, even though grip levels are low by later standards. Some road testers criticised a tendency for front-wheel lock-up during braking, and a skitteriness on

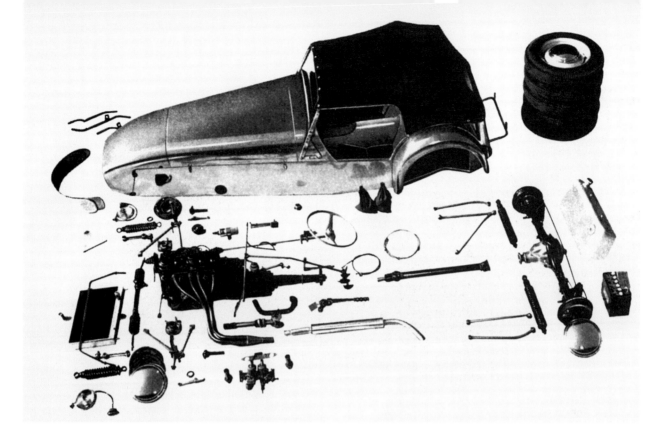

bumpy corners. This is the 7 in its purest form, unsullied by any creature comforts, bereft of weight-inducing 'extras' and a pure piece of Lotus history.

The Ford-powered car was simply known as the Lotus 7 initially, but was renamed the 7F after the launch of the 7A in October 1959. Most cars were sold as complete kits (priced at £536), but assembled cars were also offered from £1,036 including purchase tax. Optional extras included a hood, tonneau cover, windscreen wiper kit, spare wheel, wire wheels, Dunlop racing tyres, electric fuel pump, adjustable steering column with leather rim wheel, twin SU carburettors and four-branch manifold, and close-ratio gears.

It is not known how many of the Series 1 7s were fitted with the Ford engine, but this powerplant's popularity was such that the sidevalve continued to be offered in the Series 2 when it was launched in June 1960.

The 7 was unusual in that every item needed to complete the car was included in the kit. Despite this, its price was very low and it achieved instant popularity.

Summary

The original 7 in its pure, unadulterated form was a stroke of Chapman genius, but asthmatic Ford engine seems ludicrously underpowered these days.

Identifying features

Ford sidevalve engine and three-speed gearbox, all-aluminium bodywork, chassis number sequence 400–499 (Hornsey built), and 750–892 (Cheshunt built).

There was very little to the 7's cabin, with enough space for a speedometer in front of the driver, three minor gauges and a dash-mounted fuse box. The handbrake sat in the passenger footwell.

Super 7C Series 1

Reaching a Climax

With the Coventry Climax engine fitted, the 7 became the Super 7 (also known as the 7C). In this guise it was a much more serious tool.

Specification	
Engine	Coventry Climax FWA 1100
Capacity	1,098cc
Bore x stroke	72.4 x 66.6mm
Induction	Twin SU H2 carburettors
Compression ratio	9.8:1
Max power	75bhp (56kW) at 6,250rpm
Max torque	Not quoted
Gearbox	Austin A30 four-speed
Brakes	8in drums front and rear
Steering	Modified Morris Minor rack-and-pinion
Weight	924lb (419kg)
Top speed	104mph (167kph)
0-60mph	9.2sec
50-70mph	6.5sec (through the gears)
Number produced	see 7F

The very first Lotus 7 was built for racing driver Edward Lewis in September 1957. Its exotic specification of Lotus 11-based brakes and de Dion rear axle could not be reproduced for road use, but Lotus certainly felt there was a need for more power. Lewis's prototype 7 boasted a Coventry Climax 1100 engine and immediately proved itself in competition, for example, scoring maiden class victories at the 1957 Brighton Speed Trials and at Prescott. The Climax-engined 7 was undoubtedly the ideal choice to compete under the Team Lotus banner in sprints and hillclimbs.

Naturally, other racers wanted a 7 fitted with the Climax engine to compete in events other than the 1172 Formula. So, in February 1958, Lotus announced the very first of a series of 'Super' 7s. The Super 7 was often referred to as the 7C by dint of its fitment of the favoured Climax engine.

Compared with the wheezy Ford sidevalve, the Climax FWA single overhead cam engine was a racer's dream. Derived from a Coventry Climax standing fire-pump unit, it was high-revving, relatively light (thanks to its lightweight all-alloy construction) and extremely powerful for its day. An output of 75bhp at 6,250rpm was quoted for the engine, which was fitted with twin SU carburettors and a four-branch exhaust manifold. The 7 had been transformed into a genuine 100mph sports car with phenomenal

SPECIFICATION

	SEVEN 'F'	SEVEN 'A'
MODEL		
FRAME	Multi-tubular space frame comprising 1 in. and ¾ in. square and round tubing of 18 gauge steel. The propeller shaft tunnel and floor are stressed members forming an integral part of the frame. The tunnel carries the rear engine mounting. The engine is carried on two rubber mountings at the front and a single rubber mounting at the rear around the gearbox.	
FRONT SUSPENSION	Independent by transverse wishbones incorporating anti-roll bar. Springing by combined coil spring damper units reacting through a single attachment point at each end.	
REAR SUSPENSION	Proprietary live rear axle located by twin parallel trailing arms and a diagonal member to provide lateral location. Springing by combined coil spring damper units.	
BRAKES	Hydraulically operated two leading shoe drum brakes. Cast iron drums 8 in. x 1¼ in. diameter at front and rear. Combined master cylinder and hydraulic fluid reservoir serving front and rear brakes. Horizontally mounted hand brake operating rear brakes through mechanical linkage.	
STEERING	Lotus modified proprietary rack and pinion, universally jointed steering column and 16 in. 2-spoked wheel.	
POWER UNIT	Ford 100E 1,172 c.c. side-valve four-cylinder engine.	Minor 1000 or A35 948 c.c. overhead valve 4-cylinder engine.
TRANSMISSION	Single dry-plate clutch. Ford 3-speed gearbox with the following standard ratios: first 3.664:1 second 2.007:1, top 1:1; reverse, 4.79:1. Close ratios at extra cost.	B.M.C. 4-speed gearbox synchromesh on 2nd 3rd and 4th with the following ratios: first, 4.08:1; second, 2.58:1; third, 1.44:1; top 1:1; reverse, 5.17:1. Close ratios at extra cost. Single dry-plate clutch.
FINAL DRIVE	Hypoid final drive unit. Standard ratio 4.22:1. Following axle ratios available at option: 5.375, 5.125, 4.875, 4.55, 4.22, 3.89 and 3.73:1	
COOLING SYSTEM	Ultra lightweight fin and tube radiator with integral header tank.	
FUEL SYSTEM	Single light alloy rear tank 7-gallon capacity. A.C. engine mounted fuel pump.	
BODYWORK	Two-seater bodywork with exposed wheels and separate wings. Dash and cowl readily removable for access to back of instrument panel and front suspension respectively. Dash panel covered to match upholstery. Full-width glass screen is standard, but small sporting perspex screen available as optional extra.	
ELECTRICAL SYSTEM	Special lightweight 12 volt 31 amp hr. battery, weighing 24lb. located at rear. Coil and distributor, centrifugal advance and retard, belt-driven dynamo, automatic voltage control. Fuse box mounted behind dash panel. Lucas 6 in. headlamps and separate side lamps, twin stop tail lights and number plate lamp. High frequency horn. Instrument lighting	
INSTRUMENTS	3 in. speedometer 0-120 m.p.h. with combined revolution readings in the gears. Oil pressure gauge, water temperature gauge and ammeter.	
WHEELS AND TYRES	Bolt-on 15 in. lightweight wheels front and rear, all fitted with 5.20 x 15 tyres. Provision for spare wheel on rear panelling.	
DIMENSIONS	Wheelbase 7ft. 4 in. Front track 3ft. 11 in., rear track 3ft. 10½ in. Overall length 11ft. Overall width 4ft. 5 in. Height to top of scuttle 27½ in. Minimum ground clearance 5 in.	
WEIGHT	918lbs.	896lbs.

Manufactured by :
LOTUS COMPONENTS, *DELAMARE ROAD, CHESHUNT, HERTS.*
Telephone : Waltham Cross 26181

Provision is made for initial installation of the following power units and by means of interchangeable mounting brackets. Either alternative may be substituted at a later date in the life of the car.

Seven 'A' Austin A35 or Morris Minor 1000 overhead valve engine with four speed gearbox.

Seven 'F' Ford 100E side valve engine with three speed gearbox.
(N.B. The Coventry Climax 1100cc engine with Lotus close ratio gearbox may also be installed if desired—**Seven 'C' Model**).

To those who have never before driven a Lotus, the first impression on taking the wheel is one of superb driver control—instant reaction to every command.
The inherent safety of the Seven, maintained at all speeds and under extreme road conditions, enables the exhilarating performance to be confidently used to the full—high average speeds in comfort; relaxed driver.
Although successfully used in all forms of motoring competition, and race-bred in the Lotus tradition, the Seven is first and foremost a high-speed touring sports car. Full weather equipment is available and hand luggage may be stowed behind the seats. Light weight and overall mechanical efficiency result in exceptional fuel economy and negligible maintenance costs.

This publicity material (with Colin Chapman at the wheel of the 7) includes details of the 7F (Ford) and 7A (BMC), and makes mention of the more specialised 7C Climax-powered car.

acceleration for its cost. It certainly helped that the car weighed less than the 7F too.

The other most important change for the Super 7 was the fitment of a four-speed gearbox in place of the Ford three-speeder. Derived from the Austin A30, it too was offered with close-ratio gears as an option, while the standard final drive was a slightly longer 4.55:1. In fact, several axle ratios were available for the Super 7, as with the 7F.

Minor specification changes over the lesser Ford-powered 7 included an adjustable steering column with a three-spoke leather-rimmed steering wheel (the 7F had a two-spoke plastic item), a rev-counter sited in front of the driver as standard, and usually 15-inch knock-on wire wheels (as fitted to the Climax-engined Lotus Elite) in place of pressed steel.

Road tests praised the 'smoothness and willingness to rev' of the Climax engine, and how much better the four-speed gearbox was suited to the spread of power. Acceleration was now excellent, with a 9.2 second 0–60mph time. 'The Climax unit runs up to and past 7,000rpm with never a murmur of complaint,' said *Autosport* magazine, praising the 'wonderful reserve of power' and concluding it was 'an absolute joy'.

Having been announced in February 1958, in typical Lotus fashion at the time, it took until December 1958 for the first car to be built (and this car was raced by Graham Hill, one of many illustrious racers who cut their teeth on the 7). Almost all Super 7s were built while Lotus was still based in Cheshunt.

The Super 7 was sold in kit form for £700, some £120 more than the 7F. Complete cars were nominally available but very few people wanted to pay almost double for the privilege of driving a Lotus-built car away. It was said that the engine alone accounted for almost half the cost of the Super 7.

Summary

Ultra-desirable high-performance version of the original 7 with the fabulous Climax FWA engine – quickest of the Series 1 cars.

Identifying features

Coventry Climax FWA 1100 engine, all-aluminium bodywork, almost all were Cheshunt-built (in the chassis range 750–892).

The rare, powerful and free-revving Coventry Climax FWA engine is absolutely the engine to have in a 7 Series 1, but its fragile nature and extraordinary rebuild costs consign it to a very rarefied audience.

7A Series 1

BMC power ideal for the US market

A more modern alternative to the Ford sidevalve engine was the BMC A-series unit, as fitted to the Austin A35 and Morris 1000. This one has twin carburettors, which were standard on 7As sold in the USA.

By 1959, Lotus was becoming a very well-known name by virtue of its competition exploits. Chapman had moved the factory from cramped premises in Hornsey to a more spacious location in nearby Cheshunt and was keen to cash in on the growing reputation of the Lotus name. He duly targeted the American market.

Amazing as it may seem now, in the 1950s, Austin was the biggest-selling import in the USA and had an enviable name over there. The Austin-Healey brand was treated with reverence and the newly launched Sprite was gaining a big following. Lotus already had an Austin connection because the 7 used a Metropolitan rear axle and the Super Seven was fitted with an A30 gearbox. All these factors led Chapman to choose the BMC A-series engine as the ideal unit for export to America.

In fact, the so-called 7A was launched in Britain first, with an engine taken directly from the Austin A35 and Morris 1000. This had a single SU carburettor and a power output of 37bhp, which may have been the lowest of any engine ever fitted to a 7, but it represented an advance on the sidevalve Ford engine because of its more eager rev band.

For the US market a twin-carb engine – basically the Austin-Healey Sprite unit – was selected, whose power rose to 43bhp. In this form the 7A was considerably quicker than the 7F and much more suited to its target market.

Summary

With BMC A-series power the 7A was more effective on the road than the 7F, although it was hardly any more romantic.

Identifying features

BMC A-series power, US-market cars have flared glassfibre front wings. All 7As were Cheshunt-built (in the chassis range 750–892).

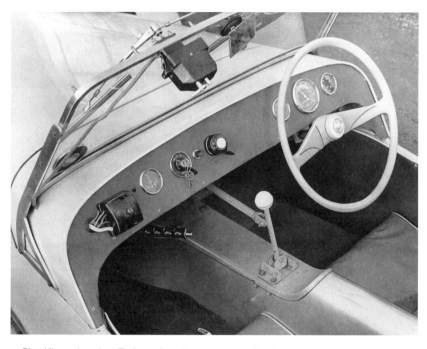

Specification	
Engine	Austin A35/Morris 1000 A-series
Capacity	948cc
Induction	Single SU (7 America twin SU)
Compression ratio	8.9:1 (7 America 8.3:1)
Bore x stroke	62.94 x 76.2mm
Max power	37bhp (27kW) at 4,800rpm (7 America 43bhp (32kW) at 5,200rpm)
Max torque	50lb ft (68Nm) at 2,500rpm (7 America 52lb ft (70Nm) at 3,300rpm)
Gearbox	Austin A30 four-speed
Brakes	8in drums front and rear
Steering	Modified Morris Minor rack-and-pinion
Weight	896lb (407kg)
Top speed	85mph (137kph)
0-60mph	14.5sec (7 America 12.2sec)
50-70mph	10.3sec (through the gears)
Number produced	see 7F

Significantly, the 7 America (as it was called) boasted elegantly flared glassfibre front wings in place of aluminium cycle wings. This set the precedent for the Series 2 and all future generations of the Lotus 7. The 7 America also benefited from an enhanced specification, including sealed-beam headlamps, proper electric windscreen wipers, an electric fan and a standard speedometer (which was optional on British market cars!).

Journals praised the 'amazing cornering power' and the smooth and controllable way the tail broke away. The performance of the 7 America was significantly better than the Austin-Healey Sprite that had donated its engine.

Along with other Series 1 models, the 7A was built by Lotus Components and listed until June 1960, when the Series 2 made its first appearance.

Note the extreme simplicity of the Series 1 seat cushions, the lack of any tunnel trim and the remote linkage gear lever.

All-aluminium bodywork was peculiar to the Series 1. Wire wheels are a common and desirable feature.

7F and 7A Series 2

Simplicity and superior manners

The early years of the Series 2 saw the Ford sidevalve and (as here above) the Austin A35 engines remain, but they had been dropped by 1962. The very early Series 2 kept the front cycle wing design (below), although in glassfibre rather than aluminium, and the new glassfibre nose cone was of an all-new shape.

The problem with the Series 1 Lotus 7 was that it was too labour-intensive to manufacture. For a model that was providing vital income for the emerging racing giant, this was a serious problem. No less than 60 man-hours were required to create a 7 kit, while the farmed-out chassis (made by Progress Chassis) was simply too complex and costly.

Colin Chapman therefore elected to remove as many chassis tubes as possible, including the engine bay diagonals, cockpit side diagonals, some of the seat back tubes and the transmission tunnel rear hoop. This naturally compromised rigidity – some thought excessively, which was typical of Lotus's current approach to weight reduction at all costs – although Chapman regained some lost strength by riveting the inner body panels and dashboard in place.

The suspension was completely revised. At the rear, an A-frame was now used to locate the axle, which changed to a Standard Companion item. The front suspension uprights now came from the Triumph Herald, and the same car donated

its steering rack, mounted ahead of the axle line. The old 15-inch wheels of the Series 1 shrank to 13 inches in diameter and were in steel only, with no wire wheel option. The standard choice was 13 x 3½-inch Dunlop wheels with crossply tyres. At extra cost one could order Dunlop R5 racing tyres and, later on, 13 x 4½-inch Lotus Elan wheels.

Other changes under the skin included a cut-down floorpan (the Series 1 had a floorpan that stretched underneath the engine and behind the cockpit to the tail – the Series 2 made do without either of these extensions), a bigger steel fuel tank (the 5½-gallon rear-sited fuel tank grew to 8 gallons from April 1962) and a battery relocated from the rear end to the engine bay.

Externally, the Series 2 was significantly changed. While cycle front wings were available for 1960 and 1961, they were now in glassfibre rather than aluminium. In any case, most owners opted for the handsome new American-style flared glassfibre front wings, setting a trend that remained in force for decades (ironically customers for the latest Caterhams favour cycle wings). The rear wings were also reprofiled and made flatter and wider, and moulded in glassfibre, while the nose cone was reshaped with a less droopy look and also made of glassfibre in either red, green or yellow (although other colours appear to have been made also). Wider rear wings were available later on to accommodate wider wheels and tyres. Inside, the inner side trim and dashboard panel came with Vynide ready bonded in place.

As for the engine choice, that remained either BMC A-series (7A) or Ford sidevalve (7F) at the time of the Series 2's launch in June 1960. However, the 7 America continued to enjoy the Austin-Healey Sprite powerplant, initially in 948cc form as before but also in expanded 1,098cc guise. *Road & Track* drove a 948cc 7 America, describing it as 'the least practical but most enjoyable sports car that we have driven'. It liked the 'quite dashing' new front wing design and praised the 'nice controllable understeer'. Back-to-back with the Elite and Lotus Junior, the magazine reported that, 'even in that sort of company the 7 is quite impressive . . . It makes the sort of standing start that we dream about . . . All in all, we were tremendously impressed.' But there was no hiding from the grossly under-powered nature of either powerplant.

The kit price was as low as £499 for a 7F in January 1961 ($2,897 for the 7 America), but both the BMC A-series and Ford sidevalve engines were quickly dropped in favour of the new Ford 105E Anglia unit (see next entry).

Summary

Much revised Series 2 Lotus 7 gains lightness at the expense of a loss of rigidity, and establishes the classic 7 look that persists to this day.

Identifying features

Revised chassis, riveted side panels and dash, usually glassfibre wings and nose, Austin/Ford engine, chassis number sequence SB1000–SB2101 (Cheshunt built) and SB2102–SB2310 (Hethel built), later left-hand drive cars have SBL or LSB prefixes.

Specification

Engine	Ford 100E sidevalve/BMC A-series
Capacity	1,172cc/948cc (7 America also 1,098cc)
Bore x stroke	63.5 x 92.5mm/62.94 x 76.2mm (7 America 1100 64.5 x 83.8mm)
Induction	Single Solex/single SU carburettor (7 America twin SU)
Compression ratio	8.5:1/8.9:1 (7 America 1100 8.9:1)
Max power	40bhp (30kW) at 4,500rpm/37bhp (27kW) at 4,800rpm (7 America 1100 55bhp (41kW) at 5,500rpm)
Max torque	52lb ft (70Nm) at 2,500rpm/50lb ft (68Nm) at 2,500rpm (7 America 52lb ft (70Nm) at 3,300rpm, 7 America 1100 61lb ft (83Nm at 2,500rpm))
Gearbox	Austin-Healey Sprite four-speed
Brakes	8in drums front, 7in drums rear
Steering	Triumph Herald rack-and-pinion
Weight	960lb (435kg)
Top speed	81mph/85mph (120kph/137kph)
0-60mph	17.8sec/14.3sec
50-70mph in top	16.5sec/8.8sec (through the gears)
Number produced	Approx 1,310 (all Series 2)

Lotus 7F and 7A Series 2 (1960–1961)

While the Series 1 chassis had been lightweight, the Series 2 went even further after Colin Chapman removed some chassis tubes. The suspension was completely revised and the wheels were reduced in diameter to 13 inches.

7 105E Series 2

New generation Ford power is a leap forward

By 1962, the Series 2 had switched to flared front wings, as fitted to early American 7s, and was widely regarded as being a better-looking and more practical car.

Summary
105E engine becomes the new base-model 7 but tuning is required to get the best performance from this power unit.

Identifying features
Glassfibre wings and nose, S2 chassis, Ford 105E engine, chassis number sequence SB1000–SB2101 (Cheshunt built) and SB2102–SB2310 (Hethel built).

Ford launched its Anglia 105E in Britain in 1959. Undoubtedly the best feature of the odd Z-back styled budget car was its engine. An oversquare 997cc overhead-valve four-cylinder unit, it was both strong and eminently tuneable. Lotus had its eyes set on this powerplant from the outset and trial-fitted one in a Series 2 chassis in late 1960 in time for a January 1961 launch, at which time the basic kit price of the car was slashed to just £499.

The 105E-engined 7 was set to become the new 'entry-level' car for the whole of the Series 2's life. It replaced at a stroke both the BMC A-series and the unpopular Ford sidevalve. In the 7 it was converted to run on twin SU carburettors, but even so its power output of 39bhp at 5,000rpm was hardly the stuff of legends. The 105E unit was frankly not a great performer and was unloved by Lotus engineers as it tended to run out of steam much beyond 70mph.

Tuned engines were naturally top of any 105E-powered 7 buyer's list. A Cosworth version with Weber carburettors and a four-branch exhaust manifold was marketed by Lotus and many after-market conversions were available.

It might be thought an advantage that the 105E powerplant came with the Ford four-speed gearbox, but first and second gears were really too slow for a sports car, and the gap between second and third was cavernous. At least in the 7 the Ford 'box had a Triumph remote control unit attached to it to give comfortable and precise gearchanges.

The Series 2 settled into a production stride of around seven cars per week during the early 1960s. Throughout the Series 2's production life there was very little in the way of development and Lotus Components simply churned out the kits. A shot in the arm was definitely given in 1965 with the car's appearance in the classic TV series *The Prisoner*, and suddenly Lotus 7s started being ordered in green with yellow nose cones. However, the following year (1966) Lotus moved premises once again, from Cheshunt to Hethel in Norfolk. Lotus informed Graham Nearn of Caterham Cars (then the main Lotus 7 distributor) that production was unlikely to restart, so Nearn promptly came up with 20 orders, which thankfully for all concerned, kept production going!

In 1961, Lotus adopted the more recent Ford Anglia 105E powerplant. Although it boasted only 997cc and was not liked by Lotus engineers, it was an engine that could be easily tuned.

Specification	
Engine	Ford 105E
Capacity	997cc
Bore x stroke	80.96 x 48.4mm
Induction	Twin SU H2 carburettors (Weber on Cosworth version)
Compression ratio	8.9:1
Max power	39bhp (29kW) at 5,000rpm
Max torque	53lb ft (72Nm) at 2,700rpm
Gearbox	Ford 105E four-speed
Brakes	8in drums front, 7in drums rear
Steering	Triumph Herald rack-and-pinion
Weight	952lb (432kg)
Top speed	83mph (133.5kph)
0-60mph	14.8sec
50-70mph in top	13.6sec
Number produced	1,350 (all Series 2)

Super 7 Cosworth 1340

With Cosworth power, a legend is born

Cosworth power revived the Super 7 name in 1961. This is the Super 7 1340 Cosworth pictured on road test with *Autocar* magazine in that year, with its rudimentary soft-top erected.

Summary

With Cosworth modifications, Ford's 1,340cc 109E Classic engine becomes an untemperamental powerhouse for the new Super 7.

Identifying features

109E engine with sand-cast Cosworth rocker cover, all chassis numbers within the sequence SB1000–SB2101.

While the new Ford Anglia 105E engine was certainly an advance on the old sidevalve, the Lotus 7 still craved a more powerful powerplant. A new Super 7 was definitely needed, but the Series 2 chassis could not use the Coventry Climax FWA as fitted in the Series 1 Super 7 because Colin Chapman's chassis modifications meant that the Climax engine would not fit (even though the first S2 adverts listed a Climax engine option!). Besides, the Climax engine was a rather expensive powerplant to buy in.

Enter Mike Costin and Keith Duckworth, who between them had founded Cosworth Engineering. As Costin was still development chief at Lotus in 1961, anything that Cosworth did, Lotus knew about. The idea of fitting the then-new Ford Classic 109E 1,340cc engine into a 7 actually came from a Lotus employee called Warren King. He used a Cosworth camshaft that worked so well that this set-up was adopted for the official 109E engine for the new production Super 7.

The 1,340cc Ford 109E engine was treated to a reworked head, Cosworth cam, two twin-choke Weber 40DCOE carburettors on a modified inlet manifold and a four-branch exhaust manifold. It was easily identified by an evocative sand-cast rocker cover bearing the Cosworth script. In this tune, the engine developed an impressive 85bhp, at the same time

38

The Cosworth-tuned Ford Classic 109E 1,340cc engine developed a mightily impressive 85bhp and was free-revving to boot. Today it is the holy grail of Series 2 engines among aficionados.

Specification	
Engine	Ford 109E Cosworth
Capacity	1,340cc
Bore x stroke	80.96 x 65mm
Induction	Twin Weber 40DCOE
Compression ratio	9.5:1 (10.5:1 in US SCCA version)
Max power	85bhp (63kW) at 5,800rpm
Max torque	80lb ft (59Nm) at 4,000rpm (85lb ft (62Nm) at 4,000rpm in US SCCA version)
Gearbox	Ford 109E Classic four-speed
Brakes	8in drums front, 7in drums rear
Steering	Triumph Herald rack-and-pinion
Weight	966lb (438kg)
Top speed	102mph (164kph)
0-60mph	6.9sec
50-70mph in top	7.9sec
Number produced	See 7A/7F Series 2

The Series 2 was usually fitted with a rev counter, positioned in front of the driver; the speedometer was repositioned on the opposite side, in front of the passenger.

All 7 Series 2s had a shortened rear undertray. Clearly visible here is the new A-frame that located a different rear axle, taken from the Standard Companion.

remaining very reliable and free-revving. An optional electric fan reduced any propensity for the engine to overheat. In America there was a special engine for SCCA racing with a higher compression ratio (10.5:1), which delivered the same 85bhp power but offered more torque.

The Series 2 Super 7 1340 Cosworth was the fastest 7 yet – a genuine 100mph car with a 0–60mph time of under eight seconds, which put it above most of the exotica of the time. It received a great reception from the magazines that test drove it. John Bolster in *Autosport* praised its 'immense punch in the middle ranges' and its 'phenomenally good' acceleration, while his performance figures were 'indications of the really immense performance of this red hot little machine.' The best 0–60 time recorded was *Sporting Motorist*'s 6.9 seconds!

As for the handling, the extra power opened up oversteer possibilities to a far greater degree, although the 13-inch wheels and tyres kept things more under control than the Series 1. Wet roads were a concern, however while braking was improved thanks to the Triumph Herald drums.

At a launch price of £599 in kit form, the new Super 7 looked superb value; an MGB in 1962 cost £834. Exact production numbers are not known, but the 1340 Cosworth is certainly a very rare beast as it only lasted from 1961 until 1962. Thereafter the Super 7 mantle was taken over by the Cortina 1500 engine (also available in Cosworth guise). The 1340 Cosworth remains one of the most desirable of the early Lotus 7 variants and highly sought after not only for its rarity but because the Cosworth badge means a lot to enthusiasts. Originality counts for everything at this level, so the more unmolested the car, the better.

Lotus Super 7 Cosworth 1340 (1961–1962)

Super 7 1500

Cortina and Cosworth for the new Super 7

With the new pre-crossflow Ford Cortina 1500 engine fitted, the Super 7 Series 2 transformed into a surprisingly docile, yet still very exciting, car.

Summary

The new Cortina engine brings extra torque and sophistication, and in Cosworth tune makes this the fastest 7 yet.

Identifying features

116E Cortina gearbox and engine (optionally in Cosworth tune with Cosworth rocker cover), rear-exit exhaust, vinyl hood, chassis number sequence within SB1000–2101 (Cheshunt built) and SB2102–SB2310 (Hethel built).

In 1962, Lotus turned to another Ford engine for the Super 7, to replace the 1,340cc Classic unit. The engine chosen – the Cortina 1500 powerplant – was the final variant used in the Series 2 and also the biggest engine yet seen in a 7.

In standard tune the 1,498cc four-cylinder engine from the Cortina gave 66bhp, which was still enough in those days for Lotus to call it a 'Super' 7. It was much quicker than the 105E-engined 7, but not much of a match for the outgoing 1340-engined Super 7.

Far more exciting was a Cosworth-tuned version of the Cortina engine. This added a fully worked cylinder head, Cosworth camshaft, higher compression ratio, four-branch exhaust manifold and twin Weber carburettors. Not only did this result in a much higher power output of 95bhp, it also gave the 7 new levels of torque (Lotus demonstration drivers would pull away from rest in fourth gear to make the point). All but the very last examples had a Cosworth rocker cover. An alternative Mk IX state of tune was available for racing (125bhp was quoted), while a fast road version with 100bhp was also offered.

The gearbox selected for the 1500 was also straight from the Cortina – an effective all-synchromesh four-speed manual – although a set of close-set ratios was optional at £40 and recommended for the Cosworth model. However, the rear axle remained the archaic and long-out-of-production Standard unit, which was now struggling to cope with nearly 100bhp, as differential failures became more common.

Other changes included 9½-inch front disc brakes from the Triumph Spitfire, and an exhaust that no longer exited at the side but extended right to the rear of the car, plus fully dipping sealed-beam headlamps and a wood-rim steering wheel. Indicators remained an option for all Series 2 models!

The 1500 Cosworth was widely tested in the press with glowing tributes all round. *Motor* magazine managed to accelerate to 100mph and back to rest again in under 30 seconds, which was unprecedented at the 7's price.

The cost was £585 in kit form for the standard 1500 model and £645 for the Cosworth, or an extra £223 fully assembled. The September 1962 launch of the 1500-engined Super 7 also saw the introduction of an optional heater at £17 10s, while an improved hood design (boasting rear three-quarter windows and now made of vinyl) also arrived at this time. It was a 1500 Cosworth model that appeared in Patrick McGoohan's TV series *The Prisoner*.

Specification	
Engine	Ford 116E Cortina/Cosworth
Capacity	1,498cc
Bore x stroke	80.96 x 72.7mm
Induction	Single Weber 40DCOE (twin Webers on Cosworth version)
Compression ratio	8.3:1/9.5:1
Max power	66bhp (49kW) at 4,600rpm/95-100bhp (71-75kW) at 6,000rpm
Max torque	79lb ft (107Nm) at 2,300rpm/95lb ft (129Nm) at 4,500rpm
Gearbox	Ford Cortina GT four-speed
Brakes	9½in discs front, 7in drums rear
Steering	Triumph Herald rack-and-pinion
Weight	1,036lb (470kg)
Top speed	100/104mph (161/167kph)
0-60mph	N/A/7.7sec
50-70mph in top	N/A/5.8sec
Number produced	see S2

With a Cosworth casting and twin carburettors, the 1500 engine transformed into a fire-breather, with 95bhp in regular form and up to 125bhp available if you wanted to go racing. It is a highly sought-after variant.

The standard 66bhp Ford 1500 engine is seen here mated with the Ford Cortina four-speed gearbox, which delivered strong performance.

7 Series 2½
Crossflow power makes its debut

The last of the Series 2 cars were fitted with a crossflow engine from the Ford Cortina 1600GT. The so-called Series 2½ launched the crossflow 7 that would last in production right up until 1998.

Summary

Interim Series 2½ model has the benefit of the new Ford crossflow engine while retaining the lightness of the S2 chassis.

Identifying features

225E Cortina 1600 engine, Standard rear axle, chassis numbers within sequence SB2102–SB2310.

In 1968, Mike Warner took over as chief executive of Lotus Components and immediately set about revolutionising both the racing and road car production wings of that operation. Lotus Components was not profitable at that time and one of Warner's plans was to produce a radical new Lotus 7. The rest of the Lotus board disagreed with him – for the moment at least.

Warner's decision was therefore to go ahead with a revised version of the Series 2, which would become the Series 3. This new S3 would be based around the new Ford Cortina crossflow engine range in a heavily revised chassis.

However, the 1600 crossflow engine was available to Lotus before the Series 3 arrived. Ford had replaced the old 1500 unit with the 1600 engine in August 1967, and so the 7 could benefit from this improved engine, something that happened before the advent of the S3. The 1600 engine boasted a power output of 84bhp, not far off the 1500 Cosworth unit then being fitted to the last of the Series 2s.

In the production logs, the first 1600-engined car was built in 1968 and was marked both 'New Seven' and 'Series 2½'. A batch of cars was then produced with the existing Series 2 chassis and archaic Standard Companion rear axle but with the new 1600 engine, and enthusiasts generally refer to these cross-over models by the Series 2½ designation. The Standard rear axle might have been kept in production, for Lotus investigated taking over the axle production tooling itself, but this was ultimately ruled out on grounds of cost, and the availability of the much more suitable Ford Escort rear axle. Realistically looked at, the last of the Series 2 models could have done with extra chassis strengthening to cope with power outputs that were well in excess of what the chassis had been designed for way back in 1960.

It is unknown exactly how many Series 2½ cars were produced, but it could not have been more than a handful.

Specification	
Engine	Ford 225E Cortina
Capacity	1,598cc
Induction	Single Weber 32DFM carburettor
Compression ratio	9.0:1
Bore x stroke	80.96 x 77.62mm
Max power	84bhp (63kW) at 5,500rpm
Max torque	91lb ft (123Nm) at 3,500rpm
Gearbox	Ford Cortina GT four-speed
Brakes	9½in discs front, 7in drums rear
Steering	Triumph Herald rack-and-pinion
Weight	1,050lb (476kg)
Top speed	102mph (164kph)
0-60mph	N/A
50-70mph in top	N/A
Number produced	see S2

The Series 2½ shared the same interior as the Series 2, with its speedometer in front of the driver and rev counter off to the opposite side. Throughout its life, the Series 2 was almost as stark as the Series 1, lacking even a fuel gauge or a heater.

7 Series 3
1300/1600

Third-generation 7 improves still further

With the new Series 3 of 1968, the 7 received an extra lease of life. The crossflow engines (1300 or 1600) were ardent if a little coarse but worked very well in the 7's chassis.

By 1968, the 7 was actually losing money for Lotus Components and a revitalised version was called for. The initial plan had been to develop a completely revised car, but the Lotus board vetoed the idea. Instead, Lotus elected to inject new life into the existing design, based on a proposal document created by Graham Nearn of Caterham Cars, which was by now the sole distributor for the 7. The new Series 3 was a substantial evolution of the 7 with major engine, suspension and cosmetic improvements.

By this time, Ford had replaced the old 1,500cc Cortina engine with the new 225E Kent crossflow range. Lotus had already fitted the new engine to the last of the S2 cars (see previous entry) and it was the natural choice for

The Ford-engined S3 required a bonnet bulge to clear the air filter. Other external changes included wider rear wings, a full-length exhaust and optional Brand Lotus alloy wheels.

the S3. Coming straight out of the Cortina, it was available in two versions. The first was a single-carb 1600 unit with 84bhp, which was not far short of the output of the Cosworth-tuned 1500 engine. More marginal was the second engine choice, the 1300 unit with 72bhp. In both cases, the single Weber carburettor was too tall for the bonnet, so it protruded through the top of it, the pancake air filter shrouded in a silver-painted bonnet bulge. The full-length exhaust system was revised with a silencer now placed under the front wing, while an electric fan was standard for Series 3 cars.

Other than the engine, the biggest single change under the skin was the final abandonment of the old Standard Companion rear axle in favour of a Ford live axle, taken from the new Escort Mexico. Obviously this required new chassis mountings to make it fit but there was an additional challenge: it was also wider than the defunct Standard axle. Therefore the rear wings had to be widened to cover the wheels. The new axle was stronger and so more able to cope with higher power outputs, and there was a choice of final drive ratios: either 3.77:1 (standard) or 4.12:1 (optional).

To match the Ford hubs at the rear, Lotus engineered new hub assemblies up front to combine with the existing Triumph uprights. As there was a change to Ford hubs all round, this opened up the possibility of using Ford wheels. A choice of wider 5½J wheels was offered: either steel wheels from the Lotus Cortina or optional Brand Lotus alloys.

The Series 3 also marked an improvement in standard braking. The 7 now gained front disc brakes across the board (previously they had been standard on the Super 7 only), and the larger Ford Escort rear drums were far superior to the old Standard Companion ones.

Inside the cockpit, the speedometer and rev counter now sat together in front of the driver and a fuel gauge was standard for the very first time! Also, the fuel filler was on the tail panel rather than inside the boot, which was a mixed blessing; you could fill the tank without having to empty the boot, but the time taken to fill the tank grew far longer. There was also standard carpeting, while the options list now included seat belts (mounting brackets were ready-built in for the first time), a roll-over bar, heater, oil cooler, close-ratio gearbox and limited slip differential. Indicators became standard, too, the front pair mounted under the headlamps. All the electrics were now negative earthed.

As the Series 3 was some 200lb heavier than the Series 2, there was some concern about the strength of the chassis – something that would not be addressed until Caterham Cars began making the S3 in 1974. It was certainly a little whippy in Lotus S3 guise. The new axle worked well but the short suspension travel continued to give a very bumpy ride, mid-corner bumps tended to unsettle the rear end and in its 1969 road test, *Car* magazine noted that one of the A-bracket rubber bushes disintegrated under pressure.

S3 production began in August 1968 and officially ended in November 1969, the last of approximately 340 S3 cars being the Twin Cam (described in the next entry).

Summary

Significantly revised S3 is heavier but more lively thanks to Ford Kent power, has much better braking, a superior rear axle, extra comfort and more practicality.

Identifying features

225E crossflow engine, Escort rear axle, front discs, wider rear wings, external fuel filler, revised instrumentation, chassis number sequence SC2311–SC2563.

Specification

Engine	Ford 225E Kent crossflow
Capacity	1,297cc/1,598cc
Bore x stroke	80.96 x 62.99mm/ 80.96 x 77.62mm
Induction	Single Weber 32DFM carburettor
Compression ratio	9.2:1/9.0:1
Max power	72bhp (54kW) at 6,000rpm/84bhp (63kW) at 6,500rpm
Max torque	68lb ft (92Nm) at 4,000rpm/91lb ft (123Nm) at 3,500rpm
Gearbox	Ford Cortina 116E four-speed
Brakes	Girling 9in discs front, 8in drums rear
Steering	Triumph Herald rack-and-pinion
Weight	1,210lb (549kg)
Top speed	100/104mph (161/167kph)
0-60mph	N/A/7.7sec
50-70mph in top	N/A/7.8sec
Number produced	approx 340 (all S3)

The standard and by far the most common engine for the S3 was the 1600GT Cortina unit. Its 84bhp was produced healthily with a single carburettor, and it was not expensive to buy in.

Under the skin, the most important change for the S3 was its abandonment of the old Standard rear axle in favour of the new Ford Escort Mexico axle, which was wider than before.

Holbay-engined 7 remains a one-off

The Lotus 7S used a Holbay-tuned 120bhp crossflow engine. But this expensive and too-plush show model remained a one-off.

Specification

Engine	Holbay-tuned Ford crossflow
Capacity	1,598cc
Bore x stroke	80.96 x 77.62mm
Induction	Twin Weber 40DCOE carburettors
Compression ratio	10.0:1
Max power	120bhp (89kW) at 6,200rpm
Max torque	110lb ft (149Nm) at 5,000rpm
Gearbox	Ford Cortina 116E four-speed
Brakes	Girling 9in discs front, 8in drums rear
Steering	Triumph Herald rack-and-pinion
Weight	1,204lb (546kg)
Top speed	107mph (172kph)
0-60mph	7.4sec
50-70mph in top	N/A
Number produced	1

Summary

One-off Holbay-tuned 7 was a 120bhp firecracker but a tuned Ford S3 7 would have to wait until the Caterham years.

Identifying features

Holbay-tuned 1600 crossflow engine, chromed suspension, alloy dash, colour co-ordinated trim.

The great advantage of the Ford crossflow engine was that it was highly tuneable. Lotus Components already had a strong connection with engine tuner Holbay Engineering, which had been building tuned Kent engines for Lotus Formula Ford racers. It followed naturally that Components should ask Holbay for a tuned road car engine to fit into the new Series 3, whose Escort rear axle was now capable of handling a power output which was way above what had been possible previously.

The Holbay engine was based on the Kent 1600 block, adding a balanced and gas-flowed head, high-lift camshaft, special Hepolite pistons, higher 10.0:1 compression ratio, four-branch exhaust manifold and twin Weber 40DCOE carburettors. With an output of 120bhp at 6,200rpm this was easily the most powerful engine yet fitted to a 7, although the overall weight of the car played against it and it was only marginally quicker than the S2 Cosworth had been.

The new model was proudly displayed for the first time at the January 1969 Racing Car Show in London, some five months after the launch of the S3. Called the 7 S, it came with a high level of specification, including chromed suspension components, Brand Lotus alloy wheels, an aluminium dash, radio, better trim, full wool carpeting, seat belts, contoured seats, padded side panels, heater, air horns, leather steering wheel, special paintwork and colour co-ordinated gear lever and soft top. Lotus called it the 'ultimate' 7.

It was offered for sale at £1,285 in kit form or a whopping £1,600 fully built (more than a Jaguar 240). Although only the single show car was ever built, several S-type engines were built and some of the options of the S were fitted to customers' cars. The place of the 'ultimate' 7 would, some nine months later, be usurped by the Twin Cam SS, which achieved a very limited production run.

The 7 S is perhaps best regarded as the precursor to Caterham's Supersprint engine of the 1980s, another very successfully tuned version of the Kent engine which became almost the seminal powerplant for the 7 during its 15-year tenure.

7 Twin Cam SS

Lotus shoehorns the Twin Cam into the 7

Undoubtedly the most collectible 7 Series 3 is the Twin Cam SS, of which just 13 were officially made in 1969 only. Rarity and the genuine Lotus engine give it a special kudos.

Summary

Ultra-rare and ultra-quick Lotus, highly desirable because of its rarity; although a Caterham Twin Cam is a better and cheaper all-round bet, the SS is the collector's piece.

Identifying features

Twin-cam engine, recessed rear lights, rocker switches, chassis number sequence SC2564TC–SC2576TC.

Lotus had always maintained that its highly acclaimed Twin Cam engine (as fitted to the Elan and Lotus Cortina) would not fit into the 7's engine bay – which had, after all, been designed for Ford sidevalve power. Therefore Lotus always denied that it could produce a 7 Twin Cam. However, a customer who made himself known to Caterham Cars proved otherwise by installing a Twin Cam engine himself. Lotus Components took a look and decided to engineer a production version.

The main change other than the engine was to stiffen the Series 3 chassis. High-powered engines were already causing problems with snapped chassis tubes, so the opportunity was taken to firm things up. Extra triangulation was added in the engine bay and along the sides, making the chassis stronger but heavier. The prototype was even heavier than normal, as it had steel chassis panelling rather than aluminium, but all production cars had the lighter aluminium.

The Twin Cam engine was a tight fit but a natural in the 7, and the resulting model was named the Twin Cam SS. The Lotus Special Equipment version of the engine developed 115bhp, while the Holbay-assembled 'Big Valve' engine with its special camshafts developed 125bhp. As launched at the October 1969 Motor Show, it also had recessed Britax rear light clusters and indicators mounted on the nose cone, but not all SS models had such

47

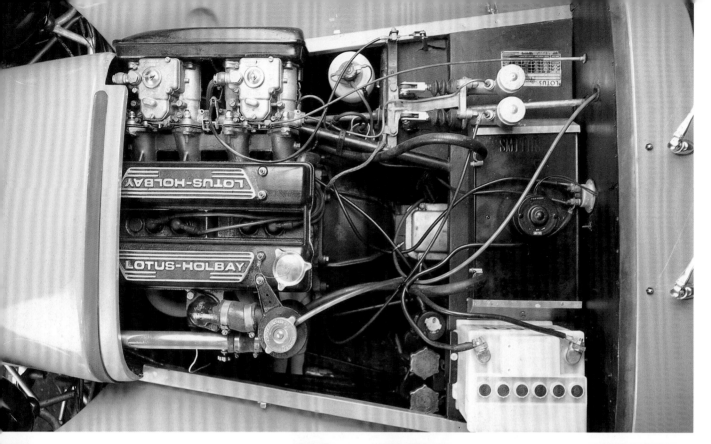

Lotus was persuaded that its own Twin Cam engine would fit into the 7 – which it did, of course. As well as the 115bhp standard Twin Cam, a Lotus Holbay version was offered with an extra 10bhp.

On the road, the new Twin Cam SS was a transformed beast, even though contemporary road tests revealed disappointing performance figures. The Twin Cam powerplant was both flexible and powerful.

Special badging identified the last baker's dozen of the Series 3 cars, all of which were Twin Cams.

a lighting arrangement. There was a return to the earlier side-mounted silencer, complete with a perforated shroud. Another change was better interior trim, plus rocker switches on the dash. The prototype also had unique Brand Lotus alloy wheels.

Contemporary road tests returned disappointing results. *Autocar* recorded a 0–60mph time of 7.1 seconds, and a top speed of 103mph. But the fact was that the SS was heavier than the standard Series 3, which dulled things slightly, and *Autocar* managed to buckle the rear locating A-frame on its test. The engine was always flexible but at its best at high revs, and there was enough power to produce rear-end breakaways virtually at will, but grip was very good if you didn't overcook things. And of course, the lightning-sharp steering was always there to help you through. *Road & Track* magazine said: 'Given the right conditions, the 7 will out-corner anything you'll ever meet.' One slightly disappointing factor was the exhaust

Specification	
Engine	Lotus Twin Cam/Lotus Holbay Twin Cam
Capacity	1,558cc
Bore x stroke	82.6 x 72.8mm
Induction	Twin Weber 40DCOE carburettors
Compression ratio	9.5:1
Max power	115bhp (86kW) at 5,500rpm/125bhp (93kW) at 6,200rpm
Max torque	108lb ft (146Nm) at 4,500rpm/116lb ft (157Nm) at 4,500rpm
Gearbox	Ford Cortina 116E four-speed
Brakes	Girling 9in discs front, 8in drums rear
Steering	Triumph Herald rack-and-pinion
Weight	1,258lb (570kg)
Top speed	110mph (177kph)
0-60mph	7.1sec
50-70mph in top	8.1sec
Number produced	13

As launched, the rear lights were recessed Britax clusters and the front indicators were mounted on the nose cone, but not all SS models were so equipped.

note, described as a 'hiss' by more than one magazine.

The launch price was £1,225 in kit form but the S3 only had one more month's production life left. As such, the Twin Cam SS was an extremely rare bird: the 13 orders taken at the Motor Show were honoured and that was that as far as the Twin Cam was concerned – and indeed these were the very last S3s built. The engine would be fitted to the 7 S4 and of course Caterham's revived S3, and many individuals have converted their Lotus 7 to Twin Cam power (and even, reportedly, Lotus Components was tempted to do the same over the coming years). Nevertheless, only 13 genuine Twin Cam SS examples were ever made, making this the most sought after of all Lotus 7s.

If you are interested in a Twin Cam-powered S3, you are much more likely to come across a Caterham-built car from the 1970s and early 1980s. Caterhams also benefit from a stiffer chassis – the Lotus S3 SS frame is widely regarded as not really being up to the job, despite its extra stiffening.

The Twin Cam SS got a special dash with gauges clustered in front of the driver, and rocker switches in place of toggle ones.

7 Series 4
1300/1600GT

Controversy and comfort

A 7 for the '70s: the Series 4 marked a complete change of direction for the entry-level Lotus as it made a bid for broader appeal. Larger, heavier and more comfortable, it aimed to steal MG Midget sales.

Summary

All-new S4 has controversial 'beach buggy' plastic bodywork and too many compromises for 7 enthusiasts but it does represent excellent value.

Identifying features

Glassfibre body, steel-panelled chassis, Ford crossflow power, Corsair gearbox, chassis number sequence 2650–3238.

'My God, they've built a new car!' was reputedly Colin Chapman's reaction on the unveiling of the Series 4 in a hangar at the Hethel factory in October 1969. While it may seem unlikely that Chapman would have had no involvement in the development of the new 7 (despite the fact that this was a Lotus Components 'secret' project), there is no doubt that the 7 Series 4 sent shock waves through Lotus and caused controversy among enthusiasts.

In March 1969, the head of Lotus Components, Mike Warner, had been given a penny-pinching £5,000 budget to design an all-new 7 for the '70s. The intention was to broaden the appeal of the 7, taking it into volume territory occupied by the ever-popular MG Midget and Triumph Spitfire. The new 7 was also meant to be significantly cheaper to produce, as Warner had estimated that Lotus was losing up to £110 on each S3 built.

Everything on the new 7 (which had its own Lotus type number – Type 60) was completely new. Created by Peter Lucas, the all-new spaceframe chassis incorporated steel cockpit and engine bay panels and a folded steel front crossmember.

While previous 7s had relied on aluminium panelling, the new chassis depended on the S4's glassfibre body for much of its strength. The cockpit and tub and main body sections were bonded on to the chassis for strength, but this also made it very difficult to repair in the result of an accident (or later on, when it came to restoration). The rear wings, scuttle and dashboard were all integral, while the front wings and hinge-forward bonnet were separate items.

The styling was perhaps the most controversial element of the new S4. Alan Barrett was responsible for the design, which picked up many themes from the original 7 while stepping boldly into the 1970s. The new car was longer by a substantial 11½ inches but no wider or taller than the Series 3.

Even the suspension changed. The rear axle remained the Ford Escort but it was now located by Watts linkages fore and aft of the axle, and with a Series 1-style single triangulated arm, which was a stronger arrangement than the old A-frame. The front end changed significantly, with the old Lotus 12-type suspension replaced by double wishbones from the Lotus Europa. Early S4s had no anti-roll bar, but one was added for later cars. Meanwhile the steering reverted to Burman rack-and-pinion, albeit with a Triumph collapsible column.

Ford crossflow engines continued to power the entry-level 7. A 1300 engine was offered but it was an awkward fit (requiring one chassis tube in the engine bay to be removed!), and very few were sold. More popular was the 1600GT, which boasted 84bhp. With all S4 engine choices, the Ford Corsair 2000E four-speed gearbox replaced the Cortina unit of earlier models.

For the first time, a 7 came with separate seats (which were even adjustable on export cars). The moulded glassfibre dash came with six gauges, four in front of the driver and two more in a hooded centre console that also housed the rocker switches.

The soft-top was all-new, as were the more generously sized sidescreens that hinged on the windscreen frame, and which now boasted small Perspex sliding panels. There was even an optional Alan Barrett-styled hardtop and rigid doors (but this was rarely ordered). Other options included magnesium alloy wheels, a heater, roll-over bar, screen washers and air horn.

Despite its extra weight, the S4 was nimble on its toes. Road testers clocked a 0–60mph time of just over eight seconds on the 84bhp GT-powered version, plus a top speed of 100mph. It pulled cleanly away from low revs but always suffered by comparison with the more exotic twin-cam engine (see next entry).

The new suspension gave the S4 a much more compliant ride, even though it was still board-stiff compared with other cars of its day. The new structure was not quite as rigid as before, and scuttle shake was in evidence. But this did not have too adverse an effect on roadholding, which remained very neutral up to high limits of grip. Push on beyond the limits of adhesion and *Motor* magazine said: 'The car is undecided whether to plough straight on with understeer or push the tail out. The result, a rather untidy lurching motion and a lot of tyre squeal.'

The new S4 was publicly launched at the Geneva Motor Show in March 1970, where it received a very mixed reaction. While it was certainly more practical and comfortable, it had lost the purity of the earlier 7 and enthusiasts were not at all convinced by it, even at £895 for the 1600GT in kit form. As much is proven by the low values of the S4 today, but at least that makes it a bargain for Lotus lovers.

Specification	
Engine	Ford 225E Kent crossflow
Capacity	1,297cc/1,598cc
Bore x stroke	80.96 x 62.99mm/ 80.96 x 77.62mm
Induction	Single Weber 32DFM carburettor
Compression ratio	9.2:1/9.0:1
Max power	72bhp (54kW) at 6,000rpm/84bhp (63kW) at 6,500rpm
Max torque	68lb ft (92Nm) at 4,000rpm/91lb ft (123Nm) at 3,500rpm
Gearbox	Ford Corsair 2000E four-speed
Brakes	Girling 9in discs front, 9in drums rear
Steering	Burman rack-and-pinion
Weight	1,276lb (579kg)
Top speed	104mph/108mph (167kph/174kph)
0-60mph	N/A/8.8sec
50-70mph in top	N/A/7.9sec
Number produced	Approx 664 (all S4)

The S4 interior featured a glassfibre moulded dashboard with the main instruments ahead of the driver and switchgear and two minor dials in the centre console.

7 Series 4 Twin Cam

Twin Cam power an easy fit for S4

Lotus's potent Twin Cam engine makes a neat fit in the engine bay. Most S4 cars on the market today have the Twin Cam engine fitted.

Summary

With Twin Cam power the S4 is more of an enthusiast's sports car but there are problems with axle tramp and the styling is ever-controversial.

Identifying features

Glassfibre body, steel-panelled chassis, Lotus Twin Cam or Holbay engine, Corsair gearbox, chassis number sequence 2650–3238.

Having proved that the Lotus Twin Cam engine was a feasible and potentially popular fitment for a 7 with the delectable S3 Twin Cam SS, it was not surprising that the powerful Lotus-built engine should find a place in the new S4.

There were actually two Twin Cam engine options. The first was Lotus's own Twin Cam, tuned to 115bhp. The second was the so-called Big Valve Twin Cam tuned by Holbay, which was rated at 125bhp (although this is probably an over-optimistic view – Caterham later claiming 115bhp for this engine). As with the Ford-engined S4, acceleration was down on the S3 because of the extra weight but aerodynamics were probably a little better, so the top speed went up by perhaps a few miles per hour.

The premium charged for the Twin Cam engine was high – at £1,245 in component form it was £350 more than the 1600GT, with the Holbay Clubman-tuned version slotting in at an extra £20.

In other respects the Twin Cam S4 was identical to the Ford-powered S4s. That meant the all-new chassis and revised suspension, glassfibre body, improved interior and better weather equipment. Early examples of all S4s had their front indicators mounted on the nose cone, but later ones were relocated to the front wings.

To drive, the S4 was more civilised than the S3 yet still one of the great

In Twin Cam guise, the S4 was a very rapid machine for its day, even though chassis flex compromised the handling somewhat. This car is fitted with a very rare glassfibre hardtop and solid doors.

sports cars of its day. However, there were problems: Twin Cam cars suffered from axle tramp because of the power output and the inner rear wheel was inclined to lift under heavy cornering. Chassis flex was noted by several road testers, but overall the steering response and feel gave more than enough control to deal with any wayward behaviour brought about by too much speed through corners.

As many as 15 cars per week were produced by Lotus Racing and overall the S4 should be judged a sales success. On the other hand, it did not live up to Lotus's sales expectations of 2,000 cars per year and the company was beleaguered with warranty claims from owners who were not used to the 7's basic nature. The last of the 640 or so S4 7s was produced in October 1972, some 15 months after Colin Chapman had decreed that the 7 no longer had a place in the Lotus line-up.

Specification	
Engine	Lotus Twin Cam/Holbay-Lotus Twin Cam
Capacity	1,558cc
Bore x stroke	82.6 x 72.8mm
Induction	Twin Weber 40DCOE carburettors
Compression ratio	9.5:1
Max power	115bhp (86kW) at 5,500rpm/125bhp (93kW) at 6,200rpm
Max torque	108lb ft (146Nm) at 4,500rpm/116lb ft (157Nm) at 4,500rpm
Gearbox	Ford Corsair 2000E four-speed
Brakes	Girling 9in discs front, 9in drums rear
Steering	Burman rack-and-pinion
Weight	1,300lb (590kg)
Top speed	116mph (187kph)
0-60mph	8.7sec
50-70mph	4.4sec (third gear)
Number produced	see S4 1300/1600

7 Series 4

Caterham briefly makes the ill-fated S4

Caterham continued production of the Series 4 completely unaltered during 1973 and into 1974. It only came to a halt once it became obvious that parts supplies were drying up.

Summary

Caterham's S4 was identical to the Lotus version but production logistics forced it out of production within one year of launch.

Identifying features

Glassfibre body, steel-panelled chassis, Ford 1300 or Lotus Twin Cam engine, chassis number sequence S4/3501–3538.

Specification

Engine	Ford crossflow or Lotus Twin Cam
Capacity	1,297cc/1,558cc
Bore x stroke	80.96 x 62.99mm / 82.6 x 72.8mm
Induction	Single Weber 32DFM carburettor/Twin Weber 40DCOE carburettors
Compression ratio	9.2:1/9.5:1
Max power	72bhp (54kW) at 6,000rpm/115bhp (86kW) at 5,500rpm
Max torque	68lb ft (92Nm) at 4,000rpm/108lb ft (146Nm) at 4,500rpm
Gearbox	Ford Corsair 2000E four-speed
Brakes	Girling 9in discs front, 9in drums rear
Steering	Burman rack-and-pinion
Weight	1,300lb (590kg)
Top speed	100mph/116mph (161kph/187kph)
0-60mph	N/A/8.7sec
50-70mph in top	N/A
Number produced	38

In July 1971, Colin Chapman made the momentous decision to end Lotus 7 production, as the model simply did not fit into his maturing vision of Lotus. It only lasted another year in production because there were so many chassis and parts unused.

Into the breach stepped Graham Nearn of Caterham Car Sales. While Nearn was no longer the sole distributor of the Lotus 7 (that arrangement ended with the S4), he remained the greatest exponent of the 7. He secured Colin Chapman's agreement as early as 1971 that he would be given first refusal to purchase the tooling and rights to the 7, something that occurred in May 1973 at Pub Lotus in London.

Caterham could not use the Lotus name and initially set up a company called the Seven Car Co. Ltd, but everyone referred to the new car as a Caterham, so that was quickly adopted as the 'official' name – 'something that just happened', recalls Graham Nearn.

Production of the 7 Series 4 began in virtually unmodified form. Apart from a new badge reading '7' instead of 'Lotus' there was no change over the Hethel-built car. The choice of engines was slightly less, with only the 1300GT and Twin Cam being listed.

Lotus agreed to continue supplying parts, including the Twin Cam engine, but with so much of the car contracted out to other suppliers, the production logistics were nightmarish, even at the modest rate of one car per week. The writing was on the wall for the S4 and the final straw came when Weathershields, who supplied the weather gear, ran out of stock and would only entertain a big production run.

Caterham's David Wakefield suggested reverting to the S3 type which was not only easier to make but preferred by enthusiasts. After only 38 S4 cars had been built by Caterham – 30 Twin Cams and eight Ford-engined examples – production ceased in June 1974 in favour of the S3.

Only the badge distinguished the new Caterham-built 7. In any case, most owners in the early days decided to fit Lotus badges.

7 Series 3 Twin Cam

Rebirth of the late, great Series 3

Momentous, Caterham's decision may have been to embark on producing the leaner, more focused Series 3, but really there was little choice in the matter. The Series 4 was complicated to manufacture and ultimately less appealing, and its days were numbered. Caterham initially relaunched the Series 3 1974 as a 'limited edition' of only 25 cars. In reality the S3 version became the definitive 7 under Caterham.

The old Lotus 7 Series 3 chassis was upgraded to Twin Cam SS specification with the addition of triangulation in the cockpit and engine areas, as well as an extra hoop in the transmission tunnel and stronger mounting points for the gearbox and steering rack. That made it much stronger and so more able to cope with the power of the chosen engine – the Lotus Big Valve Twin Cam (as fitted to the last Lotus 7 S3s). This marked a welcome return to the Twin Cam powered old-shape 7, a car that arguably should never have been replaced by the S4 in the first place.

The engine was an awkward fit because the 'Big Valve' lettering on top of the engine fouled the bonnet and nose cone. Therefore a new nose and bonnet had to be created, both slightly loftier than before. Also, the rear lights were top-mounted Britax three-in-one units rather than the Lotus Twin Cam SS's flush-mounted lights.

The specification of the Lotus S3 was duplicated fairly closely, including

It was a stroke of genius for Caterham to relaunch production of the Series 3 in 1974. Here was a lighter, purer 7 that was easier to make and preferred by enthusiasts.

Summary
Inspired decision to switch to S3 production set the scene for Caterham's next 25 years, although the Twin Cam engine was always in short supply.

Identifying features
Reinforced Lotus S3 chassis, Twin Cam engine, Corsair gearbox, top-mounted rear lights, taller bonnet and nose cone, chassis numbers within sequence 3550–4164 with TC suffix.

With extra chassis strengthening, the Twin Cam-powered Caterham had the stiffness to deliver handling finesse that the rather whippy Lotus S3 lacked. Performance was extremely strong.

Specification	
Engine	Lotus Big Valve Twin Cam/Lotus Tall Block Twin Cam
Capacity	1,558cc/1,599cc
Bore x stroke	82.6 x 72.8mm / 81 x 77.6mm
Induction	Twin Dellorto 40DHLA (1,558cc engine alternatively twin Weber 40DCOE)
Compression ratio	9.5:1 or 10.3:1/8.5:1 or 9.5:1
Max power	126bhp (94kW) at 6,500rpm/126bhp (94kW) at 6,200rpm
Max torque	113lb ft (153Nm) at 5,500rpm/106lb ft (144Nm) at 5,500rpm
Gearbox	Ford Corsair 2821E four-speed (from 1981 Ford Escort Sport four-speed)
Brakes	Girling 9in front discs, 7in rear drums (1977-80: 9in rear drums, 1980-83: 8in rear drums)
Steering	Triumph Spitfire rack-and-pinion
Weight	1,100lb (499kg)
Top speed	114mph (183kph)
0-60mph	6.2sec
50-70mph in top	6.5sec
Number produced	313

its suspension and Ford Escort rear axle. Changes included the retention of the S4's Corsair 2000E gearbox, a Hillman Avenger radiator and different exhaust manifolds. The Caterham S3 was launched in September 1974 at a cost of £1,540, although in the early years most of the production was exported.

Enthusiasts who knew their 7s were rapturous about the new 'old' car. This became the fastest car *Autocar* magazine had ever tested from 0–30mph (in just 2.3 seconds). In third gear, every 20mph acceleration increment except 50–70mph was accomplished in under four seconds. It described the roadholding as 'marvellous' but the ride as 'diabolical'. As with all road tests, praise was heaped on the steering, which always provided complete feedback and relative lightness. One's reactions were, as ever, instinctive or, as *Motor Sport* put it, 'you don't really drive it, you think it along.'

The early Caterham chassis was certainly stronger than the Lotus S3 one, but compared with later 7s it lacks rigidity. Many early cars were supplied

The nose cone and bonnet had to be altered to make the Big Valve Twin Cam engine (with its taller head lettering) fit underneath.

without a roll-over bar (it was an option for many years), adding to chassis flex.

The Lotus Twin Cam engine looked like dying when the Lotus Europa left production in 1975 but thankfully, Caterham's contract with Lotus forced Hethel to continue making these engines. Lotus declined to produce complete engines after 1977, but continued to supply them in kit form only, with construction being handled by Vegantune. The quality of construction was variable, it must be said.

The following year (1978), Twin Cam engines had to be built up from Ford 1600 blocks, creating the so-called Tall Block Twin Cam engine with a longer stroke, resulting in a cubic capacity of 1,599cc in place of 1,558cc. As with the previous Lotus Twin Cam, the quoted output of 126bhp was probably optimistic and Caterham later revised the 'real' figure to between 105 and 119bhp.

As supplies dwindled, Caterham even attempted to make its own cylinder heads from Lotus patterns and scoured the country for used serviceable head castings to complete orders for hungry customers, but by 1981 the Twin Cam was effectively dead. The final factory-supplied Lotus Twin Cam car was delivered in 1983.

Replacement options for the Twin Cam abounded. After experimenting with two turbocharged Ford installations and pursuing the abortive VTA and Holbay engines (covered in separate chapters), various conventionally tuned Ford engines would eventually take over the Twin Cam's reins.

This advert appeared in the 1974 Lotus 7 Club magazine during the 1974 transition from S4 to S3 production.

Early Caterhams had a silver-finish dashboard, while the roll-over bar was optional.

7 Series 3
1300GT/1600GT

Ford power for the entry-level 7

Almost from the outset, the S3 Caterham was made available with the Ford crossflow engine as the entry-level 7. This is a very early Caterham, distinguishable from the Lotus S3 Twin Cam SS by its tail lights, which were mounted proud of the body.

It was not long before Caterham echoed Lotus's practice of offering Ford 1300GT and 1600GT engines in the Series 3 chassis as a cheaper alternative to the Twin Cam engine. As ever, these engines were taken directly from current production Fords. However, they were initially unpopular; the 1300 unit was fitted to just four cars in total and it is unlikely that any remain with a 1.3-litre engine. And the 1600 engine was initially avoided – who would want one when a Twin Cam was on offer for not much more money? The 1600GT did not really come into its stride until the demise of the Twin Cam unit at the start of the 1980s.

Even with mere 1600GT crossflow power, the 7 was a phenomenal performer, easily beating such performance icons as the Ford Escort XR3.

The 1300 and 1600 engines came unmodified straight off the production line at Ford and, as before, developed 72bhp and 84bhp respectively. While these figures may look pale by modern standards, they were comparable with the hottest versions of the Series 1 and 2 Lotus 7. In this lightweight frame, 140bhp per tonne was quite enough for very

Summary

Ford Kent engines assume the mantle of the entry-level mainstay of the Caterham 7 range and the 7 evolves by necessity through the 1970s and '80s.

Identifying features

Ford crossflow engine, Escort Mk 1/2 and later Morris Marina/Ital rear axle and brakes, Corsair or Escort gearbox, chassis numbers within sequence 3575–5709 with '13' or '16' suffix.

The single-carb 1600GT engine was hugely durable in the 7; it only ceased to become available in the late 1990s and a chassis can still be ordered from Caterham for crossflow engines.

strong performance. There was not quite enough power to kick the tail out in the dry, where a Twin Cam would do. In some respects the 1600 was actually more enjoyable than the Twin Cam, with better torque in the lower ranges and more docile manners in traffic. In John Miles' test for *Autocar*, he found the 1600 was actually quicker than the Twin Cam in third and top below 60mph.

The crossflow 1600 unit would eventually become the most popular engine of all in time, slotting in as the entry-level powerplant for a whole generation. Indeed, the 1600GT model remained in the line-up right up until 1992, when it was replaced by the new budget GTS version. But even that kept the good old Ford Kent 1600 crossflow engine, which actually lasted right up until 1998, when it was finally superseded by the Vauxhall 1.6-litre engine.

The specification of the 7 during the 1970s evolved gradually as various parts became difficult to obtain. First the rear axle brace was extended, then in 1975 the supply of Escort Mk 1 axles dried up and a Mk 2 axle was substituted (Mk 2 RS from 1978). This then caused problems when the new front-wheel-drive Escort was launched in 1980, and so the rear axle was eventually replaced with a Morris Marina (later Ital) rear axle which was both more compact and lighter and, with its unsprung mass, could easily handle up to 150bhp. It was located on an A-frame that now sat lower down, beneath the chassis. The drum brakes were better too, and the Morris axle had the same wheel fixings as the Triumph Spitfire front hubs, meaning that the front hubs no longer required to be modified and fitted with Ford hubs.

Another shortage concerned the Corsair gearbox, supplies of which were exhausted by 1980. Fortunately, the Escort Sport four-speed gearbox fitted without problems, with the advantage of a Caterham-devised remote control gear lever that made changing gear a less knuckle-rapping exercise. Another benefit was a lighter clutch action.

Most 1600-engined Caterhams have now been upgraded, as there is plenty of scope to tune and improve the crossflow engine. But even in this humble guise, the 7 was a giant slayer.

Specification	
Engine	Ford 225E Kent crossflow
Capacity	1,297cc/1,598cc
Bore x stroke	80.96 x 62.99mm / 80.96 x 77.62mm
Induction	Single Weber 32DGV/Weber 32DGAV carburettor
Compression ratio	9.2:1/9.0:1
Max power	72bhp (54kW) at 6,000rpm/84bhp (63kW) at 6,500rpm
Max torque	68lb ft (92Nm) at 4,000rpm/91lb ft (123Nm) at 3,500rpm
Gearbox	Ford Corsair 2821E four-speed (1981-92: Ford Escort Sport four-speed)
Brakes	Girling 9in front discs, 7in rear drums (1977-80: 9in rear drums, 1980-92: 8in rear drums)
Steering	Triumph Herald rack-and-pinion (1984-92: modified Mini rack)
Weight	1,210lb (550kg)
Top speed	100mph/104mph (161kph/167kph)
0-60mph	N/A/7.7sec
50-70mph in top	N/A/7.8sec
Number produced	4/338

1600 Sprint

Caterham tunes the crossflow engine

Caterham addressed the need for a more powerful engine to take over from the fading Twin Cam by developing a tuned crossflow engine to create the 7 Sprint.

Summary

Effective modifications to the Ford Kent engine turn the 1600-powered Caterham into a virtual Twin Cam substitute.

Identifying features

Caterham-modified Ford crossflow engine, twin Webers, Morris Marina/Ital rear axle and brakes, Escort gearbox, chassis numbers within sequence 3938–5709 with 'MK' suffix.

Faced with the prospect of losing the Lotus Twin Cam engine (supplies of which were effectively exhausted by 1980), David Wakefield of Caterham realised that something had to be done in order to avoid being left with only one engine in the line-up – the humble 84bhp Ford 1600GT crossflow engine. In the event, the Twin Cam struggled on for a few more years but Wakefield's solution to the problem was an engine that would prove to be the absolute lynchpin of the Caterham range for many years: the very successful 1600 Sprint engine.

Basing the unit on the existing 1600 crossflow engine was logical, as it was already well known in the 7 and could easily be tuned economically. Caterham staff David Wakefield, Clive Roberts and Reg Price were the men behind the tuned Sprint engine. The specification included a Cosworth A2 camshaft, gas-flowed head and twin Weber 40DCOE carburettors (rather than the Dellortos of the Twin Cam, which would not fit). Initially, the carbs sat on a Holbay manifold but soon after, Caterham developed its own manifold.

The changes wrought by Caterham netted an output of 110bhp, some 26bhp higher than the standard 1600GT engine, and the Sprint engine proved both smooth and untemperamental in use. *Car* magazine described the Sprint engine thus: 'It might look mundane, but it packs 110bhp of

Webered power to push the Caterham beyond 110mph. Acceleration is terrific.' The tuning produced a sweet and flexible spread of power that ideally suited the character of the 7.

The first Sprint was built in May 1980 and it took only three years for it to emerge as the most popular engine choice among 7 buyers. Its popularity only waned after 1985, when the even more powerful Supersprint engine came on stream. Even after the Sprint title was abandoned in 1992 in favour of the GTS (and later the Classic), the Sprint engine was kept alive. Indeed, it was only retired in 1998 when Caterham adopted the Vauxhall engine as the Kent block finally disappeared from production. In later years, Caterham sourced the Kent engine from South Africa, where it was still built for the P100 pick-up. In its final form it developed 10bhp less at 100bhp but remained a staple offering – ultimately as the entry-level powerplant – until the end.

You are most likely to find the Sprint engine in a 7 with a fairly basic specification – usually with such items as a live rear axle and four-speed gearbox, although you could fit a de Dion rear end and a five-speed 'box from 1986. The basic specification is no bad thing, and this model represents an excellent entry level if you're after a used 7; an early Sprint represents the cheapest 7 on the market. Despite its crude specification, it is a surprisingly enjoyable all-rounder.

Specification	
Engine	Caterham-modified Ford crossflow
Capacity	1,598cc
Bore x stroke	80.96 x 77.62mm
Induction	Twin Weber 40DCOE carburettors
Compression ratio	9.0:1
Max power	110bhp (82kW) at 6,000rpm (later 100bhp (75kW) at 6,000rpm)
Max torque	105lb ft (142Nm) at 4,800rpm (later 100lb ft (136Nm) at 4,500rpm)
Gearbox	Ford Corsair 2821E four-speed (1981-92: Ford Escort Sport four-speed, or from 1986 Ford Sierra V6 five-speed)
Brakes	9in front discs, 8in rear drums
Steering	Triumph Herald rack-and-pinion (1984-92: modified Mini rack)
Weight	1,300lb (590kg)
Top speed	110mph (177kph)
0-60mph	6.5sec
50-70mph in top	6.7sec
Number produced	212

A Sprint-badged Caterham was regarded as 'the one to have' during the early 1980s. Twin Weber carburettors and a Cosworth A2 camshaft netted 110bhp from the Sprint engine, later revised to 100bhp.

The 7 Sprint was an inexpensive choice, yet it never failed to impress anyone who drove it. It offered reliable performance and suited the 7 chassis ideally.

VTA

Rare Twin Cam stop-gap from Vegantune

Opposite lock antics were all too feasible with the Vegantune-engined Caterham 7 VTA (here with road tester John Miles at the wheel), which revived Twin Cam glory for a few brief years.

Summary

Understandable nostalgia for the Twin Cam engine persuaded Caterham to fund a Vegantune-produced VTA twin cam engine but ultimately it scored little success.

Identifying features

VTA twin cam engine with 'Caterham' branded cam covers and VTA numbering, twin Dellortos, Morris Marina/Ital rear axle and brakes, chassis numbers within sequence 4077–4397 with 'VC' suffix.

Since the Lotus Twin Cam engine had first been persuaded to fit into a 7's engine bay in 1969, the Twin Cam unit had been *the* engine to have in your 7. It was the most powerful engine in the line-up, boasted a willingness to rev, sounded great and of course had the cachet of being a genuine Lotus engine.

The news about Lotus ending production of the famous powerplant was a bitter blow for Caterham. Even Vegantune's efforts to keep production going using second-hand cylinder heads were now exhausted. Caterham relied on the Twin Cam engine in the increasingly important Japanese market, where they would not touch a 7 unless it had the Twin Cam engine.

So Caterham actually funded the development and pattern manufacture of a new Twin Cam replacement. Going to George Robinson of Vegantune, a new VTA powerplant was developed. Based as ever on the Ford Kent crossflow block, the Twin Cam head drew its inspiration from the Lotus, Cosworth BDA and Fiat equivalents. It also stuck with the twin Dellorto 40DHLA carbs of the old Lotus unit. As a result it sounded just right and produced even more power than the Lotus Twin Cam unit, at 130bhp. *Autocar* tested one in 1983 and found it to have an identical 0–60mph time as the Lotus version at 6.2 seconds, although in-gear acceleration and fuel economy were not so good.

For a short time the VTA engine was a useful direct substitute for the Lotus Twin Cam. But the manufacturing quality was not high, with two-thirds of all power units supplied proving to need work before fitment. Common problems included oil leaks, broken camshafts and misaligned pulley belts.

Over a four-year period only 41 Vegantune VTA engines were supplied to Caterham (with Caterham branded cam covers). By 1985 there were also Cosworth BDR and 1700 Supersprint engine options that offered more power and greater reliability, and in the Supersprint's case, a more sensible price. The days of the Twin Cam, therefore, finally ended.

Vegantune's **VTA** twin-cam engine was based on the Ford crossflow block, but used its own heads and twin Dellorto carbs for a fabulous engine note and a healthy 130bhp.

Specification	
Engine	Vegantune VTA twin cam
Capacity	1,598cc
Bore x stroke	80.96 x 77.62mm
Induction	Twin Dellorto 40DHLA carburettors
Compression ratio	10.0:1
Max power	130bhp (97kW) at 6,500rpm
Max torque	115lb ft (156Nm) at 5,000rpm
Gearbox	Ford Escort Sport four-speed
Brakes	Girling 9in front drums, 8in Marina rear drums
Steering	Triumph Spitfire rack-and-pinion (modified Mini from 1984)
Weight	1,100lb (499kg)
Top speed	107mph (172kph)
0-60mph	6.2sec
50-70mph in top	8.8sec
Number produced	41

Silver Jubilee

Celebrating 25 years of the 7

Surely no-one could have imagined – Colin Chapman especially – that a car conceived hastily in 1957 as a stop-gap money-earner would last 25 years. Indeed, Chapman was occasionally infuriated that demand seemed to keep it going well beyond the point where he would have liked to have retired it and in his own words: 'The only way we could really stop it was by closing down Lotus Components.'

It was always Caterham – and specifically Graham Nearn – that refused to let the 7 die and as we know, it lasted well beyond the 25 years of the first really big anniversary which celebrated the silver jubilee of the 7 in 1982. The new anniversary model was actually first displayed at the October 1981 London Motorfair in readiness for the jubilee year.

This was the most fully specified 7 yet produced, which makes it historic in a fashion, for it trailblazed the idea of up-market 7s with a little more attention to creature comforts – a direction that would develop significantly during the 1980s.

As displayed, the 7 had a special silver paint scheme with contrasting stripes (conceived by Jim Whiting), nickel-plated front suspension, tinted windscreen, satin-black underbonnet, grey-painted chassis and lockable fuel cap. Not all Silver Jubilee cars had the silver paint scheme – one was painted in Jaguar British Racing Green with matching trim. The show car had a 1600 Sprint engine fitted (it was then the 'new kid on the block' of the engine range), although in practice, any of the contemporary engine options could be fitted.

The Silver Jubilee package retailed for an extra £1,400, making the CKD-form 7 a premium-priced product at £7,250 at launch. That probably explains the slow take-up for the anniversary edition car, but the fact that a 7 sold at all for such an elevated price bode well for the future of Caterham. In fact, a mere seven examples were completed to Silver Jubilee specification, the last one being built in 1983, plus one further car painted in British Racing Green.

The Silver Jubilee marked 25 years of the 7. Seen here at the 1981 London Motorfair, it trailblazed the notion of an up-market 7 with its snazzy paintwork and plush specification.

Identifying features

Silver paintwork (except for one in BRG), contrasting stripes on wings and bonnet, nickel-plated front suspension, tinted windscreen, grey-painted chassis, chassis numbers have 'J' and three-digit number suffix.

Specification

Engine	Caterham 1600 Sprint (or others)
Capacity	1,598cc
Bore x stroke	80.96 x 77.62mm
Induction	Twin Weber 40DCOE carburettors
Compression ratio	9.0:1
Max power	110bhp (82kW) at 6,000rpm
Max torque	105lb ft (142Nm) at 4,800rpm
Gearbox	Ford Escort Sport four-speed
Brakes	9in front discs, 8in rear drums
Steering	Triumph Herald rack-and-pinion
Weight	1,300lb (590kg)
Top speed	110mph (177kph)
0-60mph	6.5sec
50-70mph in top	6.7sec
Number produced	8

Dress-up special from Avon Coachworks

Undoubtedly the Silver Jubilee model produced by Caterham had a big influence on the sort of specification customers started asking for during the 1980s. Increasingly, the affluence in certain sections of the population during that particular decade led to demand for previously uncountenanced items of luxury. Fancy colour schemes, leather upholstery, colour co-ordinated trim and hi-fi equipment began to make their appearance on 7s – these were the sorts of things that the 7 had originally done everything in its power to escape from. However, even Caterham was forced to accept how the market was changing.

Having produced the Silver Jubilee model, which was very much a trailblazer in this respect, Caterham was open to a request from Avon Coachwork Ltd of Warwick to produce an officially sanctioned 7 with a similarly up-market feel. Avon was perhaps best-known for its Jaguar conversions, including drophead and estate versions of the Jaguar XJ series. Avon asked Caterham if it could apply its modifications and call the resulting car the Super 7 A, and Caterham agreed.

Avon's modifications included a two-tone paint scheme (the front and rear wings were in a contrasting shade), pepperpot-style alloy wheels, far more extensive soundproofing than the standard 7, small adjustable wind deflectors placed either side of the windscreen, a fully trimmed interior

Coachbuilder Avon offered the 7 A as an up-market 7. Visible here are the two-tone paint scheme, pepperpot alloy wheels and wind deflectors.

Summary

Tarted-up coachbuilt 7 that failed to find custom via Avon, the independent coachbuilding company.

Identifying features

Two-tone paint, pepperpot alloy wheels, wind deflectors, specially trimmed interior.

(including padded trim over the scuttle) in special two-tone colours, a branded spare wheel cover and extra instruments. This raft of alterations cost the not inconsiderable sum of £1,250 at a time when the standard 7 cost under £6,000. The world was simply not ready for a 7 of this sort of specification and price. It is believed that only two cars were ever built to Avon's 'A' specification.

An incidental final word about Avon's Super 7 A: it was the very first production 7 to be fitted with the new Vegantune VTA engine, which was at that time the highest-specification engine on offer from Caterham and therefore the most appropriate for an up-market car as Avon intended.

Specification	
Engine	Vegantune VTA twin cam
Capacity	1,598cc
Bore x stroke	80.96 x 77.62mm
Induction	Twin Dellorto 40DHLA carburettors
Compression ratio	10.0:1
Max power	130bhp (97kW) at 6,500rpm
Max torque	115lb ft (156Nm) at 5,000rpm
Gearbox	Ford Escort Sport four-speed
Brakes	Girling 9in front drums, 8in Marina rear drums
Steering	Triumph Spitfire rack-and-pinion
Weight	1,100lb (499kg)
Top speed	107mph (172kph)
0-60mph	6.2sec
50-70mph in top	8.8sec
Number produced	2

A fully trimmed two-tone interior, spare wheel cover and extra instruments completed the Avon 7 A package, but at £7,250 it is not surprising that only two such cars were ever built.

7 1700 Supersprint/Holbay

Reliable power to match the old Twin Cam

The early 1980s were characterised by Caterham's hunt for an engine which matched the ability of the Lotus Twin Cam. While the 1600 Sprint engine was good, it did not approach the power output of the old Big Valve powerplant.

A stop-gap arrived in 1982 in the form of Holbay's R120 engine. This was a bored-out 1,699cc version of the familiar Ford Kent engine. Between 1982 and 1984 only five cars were ever fitted with this 140bhp unit, not because there was anything inherently wrong with it, but because Caterham developed its own 1700 engine, the Supersprint.

The Supersprint engine was initially conceived by Caterham's Peter Cooper. The crossflow's bore was taken out to 83.3mm so that the engine displaced 1,691cc, then new, Reg Price-designed valves and Clive Roberts-designed springs were fitted, along with a balanced and lightened flywheel, gas-flowed head, high-lift camshaft, twin Weber 40DCOE carbs and a high-pressure oil pump. Like the Holbay engine, it gained a higher 9.5:1 compression ratio too. The first 250 heads were hand-built by Reg Price in his dining room!

With 135bhp on tap, this engine was more than a match for the old Twin Cam's output and even ran the Cosworth 1600 BDR pretty close, although it cost some £2,000 less than the BDR.

This famous all-white Caterham demonstrator/press car showed off the sublime combination of de Dion rear suspension and 1700 Supersprint power perfectly.

Summary
Caterham's own bored-out and highly tuned 1700 Supersprint engine is 135bhp of unfussy, delightful power – a fine and highly popular powerplant.

Identifying features
Bored-out 1700 engine, live or de Dion rear axle, Mini steering rack, chassis numbers within sequence 4330–30553 and have '17' suffix (17H for Holbay engine).

Specification	
Engine	Caterham-modified Ford crossflow/ Holbay R120
Capacity	1,691cc/1,699cc
Bore x stroke	83.3 x 77.62mm / 83.5 x 77.62mm
Induction	Twin Weber 40DCOE carburettors
Compression ratio	9.0:1/9.5:1
Max power	135bhp (101kW) at 6,000rpm/140bhp (104kW) at 6,000rpm
Max torque	122lb ft (165Nm) at 4,500rpm/121lb ft (164Nm) at 5,000rpm
Gearbox	Ford Escort Sport four-speed, or from 1986 Ford Sierra V6 five-speed
Brakes	9in front discs, 8in rear drums (de Dion rear: 9in rear drums, or from 1988, 9in rear discs)
Steering	Caterham rack-and-pinion
Weight	1,300lb (590kg)
Top speed	111mph (179kph)
0-60mph	5.6sec
50-70mph in top	6.7sec
Number produced	440 to 1995

The Supersprint engine was conceived at Caterham, having a wider bore, new valves, special springs, a balanced and lightened flywheel, gas-flowed head, high-lift camshaft, twin Weber carbs and a high-pressure oil pump. The result? 135bhp.

The Supersprint almost immediately became the most popular engine in the range, thanks to its superb response. There was a very strong spread of power, although it did not truly come on song until 3,000rpm. *Motor* magazine's road test commented: 'It works best in the 4,000–6,000rpm range hinted at by the high revs at which peak torque is developed [4,500rpm].' Nevertheless, pulling away from low revs was far superior to any other contemporary engine for the 7. Put simply, the 1700 Supersprint engine was a natural for the 7.

There were other major developments around the time of the Supersprint launch. The first was the arrival of the 'Long Cockpit' chassis in 1982, initially as an option but taking over completely from the 'Short Cockpit' within 10 years. The compactness of the new Morris Marina axle meant that an extra 2½ inches of cockpit room could be created, and drivers up to 6ft 2in could now be accommodated quite happily. Individually adjustable seats also became optional at this time, although most cars from the 1980s continued with the single foam-backed bench seat.

Even more significantly, Caterham tackled a new rear suspension treatment in October 1984. The Morris Marina rear axle would not last for ever, so an all-new set-up was designed; not a fully independent rear but a de Dion axle – echoing the very first Lotus 7 prototype built in 1957. The Ford Sierra donated its differential, CV joints, hubs and brakes, and Caterham added its own de Dion tube, links, hub-carriers and driveshafts.

The tube was located by trailing arms and an A-frame, and the chassis had to be modified to carry the new diff unit.

The whole set-up was stiffer with consequent benefits on handling, although the Caterham now lost its perfect 50/50 front/rear weight distribution, as the de Dion set-up tipped the balance slightly to the rear. And because there was a better sprung-to-unsprung weight ratio, ride quality improved too. Traction was also notably improved, especially in wet conditions, while the geometry was just as easy to set up as a live axle. *Cars & Car Conversions* magazine said: 'We unreservedly recommend the de Dion option. The legendary 7 roadholding and precision are there, but the ride is totally transformed. It is not just far better than before; we would go so far as to say it is good, very good for a car of this type. It is firm, of course, but never harsh.'

The de Dion chassis became an option for the 1985 model year. It was ideal for higher-spec 7s and became the first choice of the buyer for whom budget was not the number one issue.

As for the 1700 Supersprint engine, it was a real survivor. An old favourite of 7 drivers, it remained popular even after the Rover K-series launch, and lasted right up until February 1999. For the buyer of a used 7, it remains a relatively untemperamental way to get great performance from a 7 for a bargain price, although its twin Weber set-up usually needs constant fettling to maintain the best performance.

As road testers everywhere discovered, the Supersprint offered mighty performance for a relatively low price. The 0-60mph dash was accomplished in just 5.6 seconds.

Caterham's interior duplicated the stark feel of the Lotus, although it was in fact much better equipped. It was designed – along with its owner – to cope with the occasional deluge making everything damp.

1600 BDR

Legendary Cosworth BDR makes its debut

This cut-away reveals the simple but potently effective innards of the BDR-powered Caterham.

Summary

Cosworth-tuned 1600 BDR engine turns the 7 into a true supercar-slaying road-burner and the quickest and most expensive 7 yet.

Identifying features

Cosworth BDR 1600 engine with twin Weber 40DCOE carbs, live or de Dion rear axle, chassis numbers within sequence 4268–5793 and have 'BD' suffix, engines have 'BDR' and triple-numeral suffix.

Everyone at Caterham knew the 7's chassis was quite capable of coping with much higher power outputs than were then available. Out of the blue, Cosworth Engineering's Len Newton contacted Caterham in 1983 with the unexpected news that it was putting a revised version of the famous Cosworth BDA 16-valve engine back into production, and would Caterham be interested in such a move? The immediate and obvious response was 'yes!' – after all, Cosworth had a strong historical connection with the 7, the BDA engine itself had a long and illustrious history behind it and the sort of power outputs that were being talked about would make this the quickest 7 yet made.

Langford & Peck (now Langford Racing Engines) assembled a Cosworth 16-valve cylinder head kit on to a Kent 1600 block supplied by Caterham, with Cosworth pistons, belt-driven camshaft and special valves. With twin Weber 40DCOE carburettors, an 11.0:1 compression ratio and a special large-bore exhaust system, the engine delivered a claimed 150bhp at 6,500rpm. Later, after dynamometer testing by Caterham, this figure was revised to 140bhp.

The first car to be fitted with a BDR 1600 engine was in 1983 but the engine did not become available until 1984, and not properly until the following year – by which time the de Dion rear end was on stream and

The Cosworth BDR-powered Caterham 7 was blistering in action, with a 5.3 second 0–60mph time. It has all the right credentials for classic status among Caterham 7s.

Specification	
Engine	Cosworth BDR 1600
Capacity	1,598cc
Bore x stroke	80.96 x 77.62mm
Induction	Twin Weber 40DCOE carburettors
Compression ratio	11.0:1
Max power	150bhp (112kW) at 6,500rpm (later revised to 140bhp (104kW))
Max torque	125lb ft (169Nm) at 5,500rpm
Gearbox	Ford Escort four-speed or Sierra V6 five-speed
Brakes	9in front discs, 9in rear drums (from 1988, 9in rear discs)
Steering	Rack-and-pinion
Weight	1,300lb (590kg)
Top speed	118mph (190kph)
0-60mph	5.3sec
50-70mph in top	N/A
Number produced	149 (incl kits)

became the standard fitment for the BDR. This rear end was ideally suited to the extra punch of the Cosworth engine; the Marina/Ital rear axle was really at its limit for the amount of power and (more particularly) torque that the engine developed.

The new top-of-the-range Caterham received rave reviews from the few magazines that tested it, as it boasted an amazing power-to-weight ratio of not far off 300bhp per ton. The highly tuned engine was prone to exhaust crackle and popping on the over-run, resulting in an exhilarating pyrotechnic display on the passenger's side of the car.

No doubt about it, this was a very quick and agile machine. Although no magazine ever published proper independent road test results, the BDR was capable of reaching nearly 120mph, but more importantly the 0–60mph dash took just 5.3 seconds, easily the best time yet for a production 7.

There were plenty of customers willing to pay what amounted to a significant premium for the privilege of driving the fastest production 7 yet made (the launch price was £9,000). Just under one-third of all BDR engines fitted to Caterhams were the 1600 unit, the very last of those being fitted in September 1992. The 1.6-litre BDR unit was perhaps a little overshadowed by the even more potent 1700 version launched soon afterwards, especially in the latter engine's headline-grabbing High Performance Course edition. But as an engine, the 1600 BDR is virtually as sought after as the 1700 unit.

The 1,600cc Cosworth BDR engine (as fitted to this early Prisoner edition) featured a 16-valve head, Cosworth pistons, belt-driven camshaft and special valves, plus twin Webers, higher compression ratio and a wide-bore exhaust to develop a claimed 150bhp.

1700 BDR

Bored-out Cosworth engine delivers knock-out punch

With the Cosworth 1700 BDR, Caterham moved into a new era of high performance 7s, for this was easily the fastest production 7 yet built.

Summary

Bored-out and even more highly tuned Cosworth 1700 BDR engine marks a new high for the 7 and inspires nostalgia in the folk at Caterham even now.

Identifying features

Cosworth BDR 1700 engine with twin Weber 45DCOE carbs, de Dion rear axle, chassis numbers within sequence 4519–30760 and have 'BD' suffix, engines have 'BDR' and triple-numeral suffix (last unit BDR494).

Such was the success of the Cosworth BDR 1600 engine – both technically and in terms of popularity with customers – that Caterham asked Cosworth Engineering to produce a kit of parts for an even more powerful version. This would then bolt on to a Ford block that was bored out to 83.5mm, resulting in a displacement of 1,699cc.

The new 1700 BDR engine had a very similar specification to the 1600 unit, although it did boast even more highly specified 45DCOE twin Weber carburettors. That and the extra 100 cubic centimetres took the engine to a new high in the power stakes. Cosworth quoted a maximum power output of 170bhp at 6,500rpm for the larger engine (although after Caterham tested the engine, it revised that figure to 160bhp). This sort of power was far and away the most that had ever been shoe-horned into a 7, and made a dramatic comparison with the original Cosworth-tuned 1340 engine of 1961, whose 85bhp was exactly one half of the output of the new engine.

Customers loved the magic of the Cosworth name and the extraordinary power and flexibility of the engine. However it needed to be carefully tuned in order to maintain its performance potential, and it has a reputation for wandering out of tune and spluttering all too easily. Get it right and the

The bored-out 1.7-litre version of Cosworth's fabulous BDR powerplant developed a claimed 170bhp, which equated to a phenomenal 100bhp per litre. It was the most delectable powerplant fitted to a 7 during the 1980s.

experience is like no other engine.

Caterham gained huge publicity from the decision not to sell a 1700 BDR to a customer unless they attended a High Performance Course run by performance driving instructor John Lyon. This led directly to an even higher level of specification for BDR-engined cars called the HPC, which is described in the following entry.

Another important development launched in the same year as the 1700 BDR was a five-speed gearbox option. This came about because the Ford Escort Sport four-speed 'box was becoming scarce. Out of several alternatives, Caterham selected the Sierra XR4i five-speeder which has well-spaced ratios and an 'overdrive' top gear. Re-engineering the chassis for the new gearbox led to the so-called 'universal' chassis – the same spaceframe whatever the gearbox choice or steering wheel position – which also liberated a lot of extra legroom.

Specification	
Engine	Cosworth BDR 1700
Capacity	1,699cc
Bore x stroke	83.5 x 77.62mm
Induction	Twin Weber 45DCOE carburettors
Compression ratio	11.0:1
Max power	170bhp (127kW) at 6,500rpm (later revised to 160bhp (119kW))
Max torque	140lb ft (190Nm) at 5,500rpm
Gearbox	Ford Sierra V6 five-speed
Brakes	9in front discs, 9in rear drums (from 1988, 9in rear discs)
Steering	Rack-and-pinion
Weight	1,300lb (590kg)
Top speed	120mph (193kph)
0-60mph	5.0sec
50-70mph in top	N/A
Number produced	269 (incl kits but excl HPC cars)

HPC 1700

You had to pass a special test to buy one

A special badge was created for the HPC, which was a BDR 1700-engined 7 fitted with a rear anti-roll bar, limited slip differential and adjustable seats. Only 62 were ever made.

Specification

Engine	Cosworth BDR 1700
Capacity	1,699cc
Bore x stroke	83.5 x 77.62mm
Induction	Twin Weber 45DCOE carburettors
Compression ratio	11.0:1
Max power	170bhp (127kW) at 6,500rpm (later revised to 160bhp (119kW))
Max torque	140lb ft (190Nm) at 5,500rpm
Gearbox	Ford Sierra V6 five-speed
Brakes	9in front discs, 9in rear drums (from 1988, 9in rear discs)
Steering	Rack-and-pinion
Weight	1,300lb (590kg)
Top speed	120mph (193kph)
0-60mph	5.0sec
50-70mph in top	N/A
Number produced	62

Summary

This is the ultimate 1980s 7 – very, very quick thanks to the 1700 BDR engine and with its suspension and drivetrain tweaks, even more accomplished on the road – A1 collectible.

Identifying features

Cosworth BDR 1700 engine, de Dion rear axle, rear anti-roll bar, limited-slip diff, chassis numbers within sequence 4628–30696 with 'HP' suffix, engines having 'BDR' and triple-numeral suffix.

Caterham derived huge publicity from the decision to restrict sales of the 1700 BDR-engined 7 to buyers who took a special performance driving instruction course. It was a move that echoed what Ettore Bugatti had done with the Type 57, where he accompanied you in his car to determine whether or not your driving style qualified you to own one. The move by Caterham was not merely a publicity stunt; there were genuine concerns about the ability of drivers to handle that sort of power.

Caterham's official line was: 'It takes skill and responsibility to drive safely and well and a fast car needs a special kind of skill that can only be fully developed with training. Caterham Cars does not wish to release the car to anyone who has not got the skill or experience to drive safely.' Caterham charged £345 plus VAT for the two-day High Performance Course but refunded the money when the customer took delivery.

The initials of John Lyon's High Performance Course inspired a new 1700 BDR-based model from Caterham, which was launched at the October 1986 British Motor Show. An optional package of improvements lifted the standard BDR to the hallowed HPC spec, which was first tried out on racer John McLean's car in 1986 (chassis number 4589).

The HPC package consisted of a rear anti-roll bar, limited slip differential and individually adjustable seats. A special HPC badge was created and every chassis was marked with an 'HP' suffix.

In a very rare road test of the HPC, *World Sportscars* magazine stated in 1989: 'Caterham are genuinely close to Utopia for the hardened enthusiast . . . As you eat into that slab of torque, maximum 140lb ft at 5,500rpm, and unleash the 170 horses at 6,500rpm, an inane grin fixes itself across your frozen countenance.'

This was the most expensive 7 yet produced at around the £12,000 mark and its market was always going to be limited – ultimately capped by the finite number of engines that Cosworth produced. Only 62 cars were ever built to the HPC specification and it's the model that Caterham's Jez Coates identifies as his personal choice of a future collectible 7.

Export 7 with Escort XR3i power

Even passionate Caterham fans could be excused for raising an eyebrow over the existence of the Ford Escort CVH-engined 7, for this was a model produced for export only. Further than that, though, the eyebrow may well stay raised because the CVH engine is hardly known for its dynamic prowess, in particular suffering from a reputation for being noisy and unrefined.

Indeed, Caterham tried a CVH installation as early as 1983 as the engineering team was concerned that the Kent engine may have a limited shelf life. A prototype (chassis number XLC/4240) was run with a twin Dellorto-equipped CVH engine, wide-ratio Ford Sierra five-speed gearbox and tunnel-mounted handbrake lever. Despite concerted efforts to develop an engine-mounting system, the engine sounded awful and performed disappointingly and the chassis was quickly re-engined.

Having been abandoned, the idea was resurrected when the Swiss Caterham importer (Fredy Kumschick) brought it to the company's attention that the Swiss authorities were insisting on ever-tighter emissions limits – well ahead of the rest of Europe. Caterham had little option but to fit an emissions-tested fuel-injected engine, and it selected the Ford Escort XR3i unit.

The first such car was built in 1986 and the last of a total of 91 units was produced in 1991. In 1987, Caterham tried a turbocharged version of this engine in a prototype intended for the German market. That had little future but in Switzerland, Kumschick turbocharged around 75 per cent of the XR3i engines locally, giving them a performance bite that was roughly equivalent to a Supersprint. Kumschick would later offer another 7 unique to the Swiss market in the ferocious Opel Turbo powered 7, which boasted no less than 300bhp – but that story is told later.

Private owners have attempted to fit the CVH engine into 7s in the UK (as well as numerous other engines including Ford Zetec, Alfa Romeo, Toyota Twin Cam and even Rover V8). In all cases Caterham officially advises against alternative engine installations and will not service non-factory specification engine choices. The fact that the CVH engine was fitted to the Swiss-market 7 gives it some credibility, however.

Caterham created a 7 with a Ford Escort XR3 CVH engine especially for the Swiss market, with a prototype built as early as 1983. This is the Minister Racing Engines XR3i-powered Caterham.

Summary

Export-only 7 for the Swiss market came with a Ford Escort XR3i CVH engine fitted, many of which were turbocharged locally.

Identifying features

Ford Escort XR3i CVH engine, left-hand drive only, chassis numbers within sequence 4630–5589 and having 'XR' suffix.

Specification	
Engine	Ford Escort XR3i CVH/Turbo
Capacity	1,596cc
Bore x stroke	80 x 80mm
Induction	Fuel injection
Compression ratio	9.5:1/8.2:1
Max power	105bhp (77kW) at 6,000rpm/132bhp (97kW) at 5,750rpm
Max torque	102lb ft (138Nm) at 4,800rpm/133lb ft (181Nm) at 2,750rpm
Gearbox	Ford Sierra V6 five-speed
Brakes	9in front discs, 9in rear drums (from 1988, 9in rear discs)
Steering	Rack-and-pinion
Weight	1,300lb (590kg)
Top speed	N/A
0-60mph	N/A
50-70mph in top	N/A
Number produced	91

Prisoner

A 7 especially for 'Number 6'

The Village (Portmeirion), a roving weather balloon 'policeman' and a 7 with a yellow nose cone: it could only be *The Prisoner*, the cult Patrick McGoohan TV series from 1966. Caterham cashed in on its enduring popularity with a Prisoner special edition.

Summary
Break free with the Prisoner special edition, a concoction for fans of the TV classic and the Lotus 7, with unique colours and special trim.

Identifying features
Special 'Prisoner' colour scheme (yellow and green), all-red interior including red leather seats, Prisoner 15-inch alloys, chassis numbers have 'PRI' and three-digit suffix (first chassis number 4944/PRI001).

Hear the battle cry 'I am not a number, I am a free man!' and you instantly invoke the defining phrase of the classic 1966 TV series *The Prisoner*, starring Patrick McGoohan. The car he drove as 'Number 6' in the opening sequence of every episode was a Lotus 7 Series 2 Cosworth, with the highly distinctive colour scheme of British Racing Green paint and a yellow nose cone.

Caterham Cars became involved with the TV series in the final episode when the 7 was required again for shooting. The original no longer existed, so David Wakefield created a doppelganger almost overnight, and Graham Nearn actually appeared in the final episode as the delivery driver.

Numerous replicas of the Prisoner car, which carried one of the world's most famous registration plates, KAR 120C, made their appearance over the years. Against a background of enduring interest in *The Prisoner*, it was an entirely logical step to offer an official factory limited edition version.

Naturally, the paint scheme was duplicated, as was the Series 2-style all-red interior (including red leather seats and red Wilton carpeting, plus chrome instrument bezels, chrome rear numberplate lamp and white-edged weather gear). Special 15-inch alloy wheels were cast to emulate the style of the Elan hubcap on the original wheel (although obviously the size was much bigger than the 1960s version). These wheels became a regular

Specification	
Engine	Caterham 1700 Supersprint (or any other)
Capacity	1,691cc
Bore x stroke	83.3 x 77.62mm
Induction	Twin Weber 40DCOE carburettors
Compression ratio	9.0:1
Max power	135bhp (101kW) at 6,000rpm
Max torque	122lb ft (165Nm) at 4,500rpm
Gearbox	Ford Escort Sport four-speed or Sierra V6 five-speed
Brakes	9in front discs, 8in rear drums (de Dion rear: 9in rear discs)
Steering	Caterham rack-and-pinion
Weight	1,300lb (590kg)
Top speed	111mph (179kph)
0-60mph	5.6sec
50-70mph in top	6.7sec
Number produced	47 to date

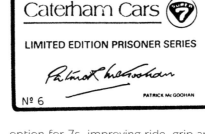

Patrick McGoohan climbs aboard his Lotus 7 S2 Cosworth 1500 in the original TV setting. All Prisoner cars came with a special, signed certificate from Patrick McGoohan.

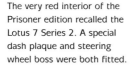

The very red interior of the Prisoner edition recalled the Lotus 7 Series 2. A special dash plaque and steering wheel boss were both fitted.

option for 7s, improving ride, grip and stability, and were only withdrawn in 2001.

The Prisoner edition was presented with huge publicity at the October 1990 Birmingham Motor Show, McGoohan having flown in specially from Hollywood to launch the car and receive the keys to chassis number 6. Other owners received a numbered dashboard plaque with the penny-farthing motif and a signed certificate of authenticity from McGoohan.

Press interest in the Prisoner 7 was intense, with plenty of opportunity to quote extensively from the series, and allude to such references as 'Rover' the weather balloon policeman. Caterham took many publicity photos of the car at Portmeirion, the highly individual North Wales location for the original TV series, including shots of the car driving along the beach.

Any current engine could be fitted (the Supersprint Prisoner was listed at £16,951) and, while the upmarket nature of the edition meant that most were sold in full component form, it was possible to order a Prisoner in basic kit form without an engine. The factory was even asked to build an R500 in Prisoner specification, which it duly did! Every genuine Prisoner car has a special 'PRI' chassis number code, but authentic Prisoner cars are very rare; just 47 are the 'real thing' with the proper chassis code and plaques (up until November 2001, when Graham Nearn's VVC-powered Prisoner was completed). Obviously, many other amateur attempts to replicate the Prisoner look can be found on the market.

HPC VX/VXI

Vauxhall power for the new HPC

Vauxhall 2.0-litre power created a new HPC legend in 1990. Huge power and unprecedented grip fused to bring about the fastest cross-country Caterham yet.

Summary

Vauxhall twin-cam engine takes the HPC spirit on to a new plane and proves reliable and tractable as well as fantastically fast – although the tyres have too much grip for some tastes.

Identifying features

Caterham-Vauxhall 2.0 twin-cam engine, 16-inch KN alloys, limited-slip diff, '7' logo on grille from 1993, chassis numbers within sequence 5253–30521 (VXI 5416–21149) with 'VX' suffix, engines have 'VX' and four-digit suffix.

While the Cosworth BDR engine was a fabulous and popular power unit, it had many drawbacks: it was expensive, rather dated, had an uncertain production future and was too unreliable for the professional class of buyers who could afford it, in an age that was increasingly coming to terms with the cast-iron performance of fuel injection. So Caterham searched around for a likely replacement, taking them ultimately to a brand-new engine supplier, Vauxhall.

The Vauxhall 2.0-litre twin cam 16V engine was an inspired choice. Not only did it keep the Cosworth connection going – Cosworth had devised and initially cast and assembled the twin cam head for GM – but it was a brilliant engine in its own right. An all-square engine, it had first been used in the 1988 Astra GTE. Very powerful and torquey, eager to rev and with an instant throttle response, it was the most rounded engine yet seen in a 7. Caterham also fitted twin Weber 45DCOE carbs on a special manifold (in place of the GM fuel injection system) to satisfy demand for good old carb-fed power. In this form a record 175bhp was extracted, and the engine was branded a Caterham-Vauxhall on the cam cover.

The chassis had to be altered again to make the big Vauxhall engine fit, with the power train sitting lower and 50mm further back. The spec also included new gearbox mounts and a new bellhousing. There was also the

Specification	
Engine	Caterham-Vauxhall twin-cam VX carb/VXI injection
Capacity	1,998cc
Bore x stroke	86 x 86mm
Induction	Twin Weber 45DCOE carburettors/Bosch Motronic fuel injection
Compression ratio	10.5:1
Max power	175bhp (130kW) at 6,000rpm/VXI 165bhp (123kW) at 6,000rpm
Max torque	155lb ft (210Nm) at 4,800rpm/165lb ft (223Nm) at 4,500rpm
Gearbox	Ford Sierra V6 five-speed or Caterham six-speed
Brakes	9in front discs, 9in rear discs
Steering	Caterham rack-and-pinion
Weight	1,300lb (590kg)
Top speed	126mph (203kph)
0-60mph	5.2sec
50-70mph in top	5.6sec
Number produced	337 to 1995

A full HPC kit laid out; while Caterhams could be purchased fully built from 1993, the majority continued to be sold in complete knock-down (CKD) or kit form.

option of dry-sump lubrication, which necessitated different sump and bellhousing castings.

Standard equipment included a limited slip differential, adjustable seats and special new KN-manufactured 16-inch alloy wheels with 205/45 ZR16 tyres. These provided much more grip than lesser 7s, which was either an advantage or a drawback depending on your driving style.

Performance was the key with this model and the VX-powered 7 had it in full measure. Caterham claimed a 0–60mph time of 4.8 seconds and a top speed of 126mph. *Performance Car* magazine did the 0–60 sprint in 4.9 seconds, while *Autocar & Motor* discovered that the HPC's 50–70mph acceleration time (5.7 seconds) was faster than any other car it had ever tested. The feel was far more rorty and raw than the K-series, and utterly rewarding. As the magazine put it: 'a rich sensory experience of total driver involvement.'

Because the engine was 16kg heavier than the Ford crossflow engine, handling was perhaps a little less sharp than the K-series 7. Turn-in was superb and the wider tyres meant that grip was unparalleled in a 7, especially in dry conditions. But when the car did let go under extreme provocation, it required razor-sharp responses to catch.

The new Vauxhall-powered 7 was launched in August 1990 at Caterham's newly acquired factory in Dartford, Kent, with Vauxhall's full support. It was an expensive beast at £18,492 but instantly found customer acceptance. The HPC label was kept and customers under the age of 25 were obliged to take a half-day High Performance Course, which was optional but recommended for drivers over 25. Not all VX-powered cars were in fact to HPC specification (which included 16-inch wheels, leather seats, Motolita steering wheel, heater and spare tyre cover).

From 1991, a fuel-injected VXI version was also offered, with either

Bosch Motronic M2.5 (M2.8 after 1993) fuel injection in place, which at 165bhp developed 10bhp less power, although it had a little more torque. This engine satisfied European emission requirements. Indeed the Vauxhall engine can be regarded as probably the most reliable route to high power in a 7: it was installed virtually 'out of the box' from Vauxhall with no internal modifications, and hence is an utterly dependable engine.

The engine fitted to the Vauxhall race series cars got Weber 48DCO/SP carburettors and developed more power, at 188bhp (140kW) at 6,000rpm, as well as more torque at 165lb ft (223Nm) at 4,800rpm.

In 1994, an experiment was carried out in turbocharging the Vauxhall engine. This ended up with 250bhp and proved far too much of a handful to offer to the public, but in Switzerland, a 300bhp 2.0-litre GM turbo engine has indeed been marketed to the public (this model is covered separately). The Vauxhall engine was replaced in 1998 by the 190bhp K-series VHPD unit, although the very last carburettor Vauxhall-powered car was produced in 1999 as a replica of the Zolder race winner for Japan.

A new HPC badge was created for the Vauxhall-powered HPC.

The twin-carb Vauxhall engine produced 175bhp with no internal modifications.

The fuel-injected VXI version may have a little less power than the carb-fed engine, but it was still a phenomenal performer.

HPC Evolution

Extra bite creates a 'junior JPE'

Virtually everyone who has ever tried the Vauxhall-engined 7 has been highly enthusiastic about it. Not only is it a powerful engine (175bhp in carburettor form), it is tractable, reliable, easy to service and good value. Not surprisingly it was a very popular choice, and remains a sought-after powerplant in used 7s.

However, the 175bhp of the standard engine was not enough for some drivers. The Vauxhall engine was temptingly straightforward to tune and so Caterham approached the best name in Vauxhall engine upgrades, Swindon Racing Engines (SRE). This company actually produced the British Touring Car Championship powerplants for Vauxhall itself and had huge experience with the 2.0-litre twin-cam unit, being the acknowledged leaders in this field.

SRE did not have to bore the engines out to extract a lot more power. Three levels of tune were offered. Stage 1 produced 218bhp, courtesy of a different camshaft with the hydraulic tappets retained, plus rejetted Weber 45DCOE carburettors, and could be identified by its blue spark plug cover. Stage 2 (at 225bhp) converted to mechanical tappets with different camshafts, rejetted carbs, and got a green spark plug cover. Stage 3 upped the compression ratio from 10.5:1 to 11.0:1, with different rejetting and had cylinder head work and an even lumpier camshaft, giving it an output

Swindon Racing Engines developed the Evolution engine packages in three stages. The cam cover changed colour with each evolutionary step up.

Summary

Swindon Racing Engines (SRE) work some tuning magic on the already-powerful Vauxhall HPC engine to produce the ferocious Evolution family in three stages of tune.

Identifying features

Caterham-Vauxhall engine tuned by Swindon Racing Engines, special-coloured (blue, green or black) cam covers, limited-slip diff, engines have 'VX' and four-digit suffix.

of 235bhp at 7,250rpm, while its torque output of 180lb ft was delivered higher up the rev band at 6,500rpm; it had a black spark plug cover. These conversions delivered very strong power outputs – and naturally corresponding performance – at the expense of some driveability.

Although there was never a factory price list for the Evolution engine upgrades, Caterham succeeded in selling about 20 sets, and it provided Caterham's engine workshop with useful trade. The Evolution engines were almost all fitted as aftersales upgrades.

The HPC Evolution models can be viewed as the 'missing link' between the standard HPC and the phenomenal JPE. Following the success of the Evolution engines, SRE also produced the engine for the JPE.

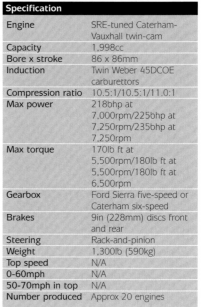

Specification	
Engine	SRE-tuned Caterham-Vauxhall twin-cam
Capacity	1,998cc
Bore x stroke	86 x 86mm
Induction	Twin Weber 45DCOE carburettors
Compression ratio	10.5:1/10.5:1/11.0:1
Max power	218bhp at 7,000rpm/225bhp at 7,250rpm/235bhp at 7,250rpm
Max torque	170lb ft at 5,500rpm/180lb ft at 5,500rpm/180lb ft at 6,500rpm
Gearbox	Ford Sierra five-speed or Caterham six-speed
Brakes	9in (228mm) discs front and rear
Steering	Rack-and-pinion
Weight	1,300lb (590kg)
Top speed	N/A
0-60mph	N/A
50-70mph in top	N/A
Number produced	Approx 20 engines

In Evolution tune, the HPC VX became a sub-JPE supercar crusher, with up to 235bhp available from various tuning modifications effected by Caterham.

Superior performance was what the Evolution package was all about – in which form the HPC was transformed into a JPE-rivalling firebreather.

35th Anniversary

Caterham marks 35 years of 7 production

HRH Prince Edward and Lord Montagu of Beaulieu in the 35th Anniversary Caterham 7.

Summary

Celebrating 35 years of the 7, the Anniversary paint scheme recalled the original Lotus racing colours, and the rest of the spec was suitably up-market.

Identifying features

Green-and-yellow paint scheme, dash-mounted plaque, Prisoner alloys, heated screen, first chassis number 5706 (fully built), last chassis number 2686 (kit-built).

Specification

Engine	Supersprint (or Sprint or Vauxhall HPC)
Capacity	1,691cc
Bore x stroke	83.3 x 77.62mm
Induction	Twin Weber 40DCOE carburettors
Compression ratio	9.0:1
Max power	135bhp (101kW) at 6,000rpm
Max torque	122lb ft (165Nm) at 4,500rpm
Gearbox	Ford Escort Sport four-speed or Sierra V6 five-speed
Brakes	9in front discs, 8in rear drums (de Dion rear: 9in rear discs)
Steering	Caterham rack-and-pinion
Weight	1,300lb (590kg)
Top speed	111mph (179kph)
0-60mph	5.6sec
50-70mph in top	6.7sec
Number produced	N/A

The 7 is one of the all-time great survivors. As each year passes the 7's appeal palpably broadens to such an extent that its momentum seems unstoppable. There is no conceivable 'end' to the 7's life. Instead, what we have is an ever-increasing catalogue of anniversaries.

The 35th continuous year of 7 production was marked in 1992 and it was felt that this anniversary warranted a special celebratory edition. In May 1992, therefore, the 35th Anniversary model was launched. Its most distinctive feature was the classic Lotus-style green-and-yellow paint scheme; the bodywork was painted all-green and finished off with a yellow stripe down the centre of the car, and the front part of the nose cone around the grille was also painted yellow. The package also included Prisoner 15-inch alloy wheels shod with fat, low profile 195/50 rubber.

Equipment levels were high. Standard items of hardware included a heated front screen, rear wing protectors, side mirrors, a heater, inertia reel seat belts, roll-over bar and full weather equipment. Every Anniversary car had a special dash-mounted plaque to prove its provenance.

Engine choices spanned the 1600 Sprint, 1700 Supersprint and Vauxhall HPC. As an up-market model, the 35th Anniversary 7 was only sold in Complete Knock-Down (CKD) and full component forms, not in kit form. Prices started at £12,999 for the 1600 Sprint version, while the component-form 1700 Supersprint cost £14,897.

The Anniversary achieved fame when an example was donated to the National Motor Museum as a raffle prize. It was widely pictured in the general press because HRH Prince Edward was pictured driving the car alongside Lord Montagu of Beaulieu.

Of course, many other 7s have since been painted in the Anniversary paint scheme, which has struck a definite chord with 7 owners (British Racing Green is actually the most popular colour for 7s). But only genuine 35th Anniversary cars with the dash-mounted plaque fetch any premium over the standard 7 equivalent.

7 GTS

Back to the 7's roots

With the GTS, Caterham relaunched the idea of a basic entry-level 7 with very few extras and a no-frills specification; live axle, four-speed gearbox, Sprint engine and a bench seat.

Summary

Low-budget 7 turns the clock back to the days of live axles, four-speed gearboxes and Ford crossflow engines.

Identifying features

Morris Ital rear axle, Ford four-speed gearbox, Sprint or Supersprint engine, simplified chassis, chassis numbers within sequence 5710–5882.

As of 1992, Caterham already had the top end of its range sorted with the new K-series and Vauxhall HPC 7s. The trouble was, this was recession time across Europe and Caterham recognised the need to address the enthusiast market – in Graham Nearn's words, 'to maintain links with the grass-roots enthusiast.' The GTS was the result.

Caterham had been pursuing a policy of constant improvement over the last two decades. While that brought great benefits in terms of the product, the new developments inevitably led to increased cost for the customer. The de Dion rear axle, five-speed gearbox and fuel-injected engines combined to make the 7 rather expensive.

The new GTS turned the clock back somewhat in an effort to achieve a low purchase price. It was effectively a relaunch of the 7 in a specification that had been fixed ten years previously. Thus the rear suspension was based around the old Morris Ital live rear axle. Because this had long since been out of production, it was a reconditioned second-hand item. The same comment applied to the four-speed Ford Escort gearbox, but otherwise the car was all-new. Also keeping costs down was an old-style vinyl-covered bench seat. Because the chassis had less triangulation, Caterham painted it in a different, Lotus 7 Series 2-style colour scheme.

The engine selected for the GTS was the Sprint unit, which by now

Specification	
Engine	1600 Sprint or 1700 Supersprint
Capacity	1,598cc/1,691cc
Bore x stroke	80.96 x 77.62mm/ 83.3 x 77.62mm
Induction	Twin Weber 40DCOE carburettors
Compression ratio	9.0:1
Max power	100bhp (75kW) at 6,000rpm/135bhp (101kW) at 6,000rpm
Max torque	100lb ft (136Nm) at 4,500rpm/122lb ft (165Nm) at 4,500rpm
Gearbox	Ford Escort Sport four-speed
Brakes	9in front discs, 8in rear drums
Steering	Caterham rack-and-pinion
Weight	1,300lb (590kg)
Top speed	110mph/111mph (177kph/179kph)
0-60mph	6.5/5.6sec
50-70mph in top	6.7/6.7sec
Number produced	approx 40

developed 100bhp rather than 110bhp. As a £1,175 option you could have a GTS fitted with a 135bhp 1700 Supersprint engine. Another option (at £455) was a Race Pack that enabled you to compete in the Class C Caterham race series.

The GTS achieved its goal of lowering prices; supplied in complete kit form it cost £8,995. Because of the reconditioned parts used in the car, the 7 GTS should be registered with a 'Q' plate in the UK. The GTS was actually very short-lived, however. It was launched in February 1992 and lasted only until October 1992. The reason was not lack of commercial success – indeed five cars per month were built – but because an even cheaper model, the Classic, took over the reins.

The GTS was very short-lived as it was superseded by the even more basic Classic.

7 Classic

Stripped-out crossflow classic cuts costs

With aero screens, no carpets, no rev-counter, no fuel gauge, no spare wheel, no heater and no weather equipment, the grass roots Classic sacrificed every luxury in pursuit of a low price.

Summary

Inspired by the early Lotus 7's pared-down specification, the Classic offers no-frills 7 thrills for a budget price, although in basic form it is hard to live with day-to-day.

Identifying features

Ital rear axle, Ford four-speed gearbox (optional five or six-speed for SE), GT/Sprint/Supersprint engine, chassis numbers within sequence 5883–30539.

The low-cost GTS had been a sales success but when Caterham's Andy Noble was flicking through a book, he saw an advert for the original Lotus 7 and surmised that it was so cheap because there was 'almost nothing to it'. So he conceived an even more stripped-out 7 that harked back to the early days of the Lotus 7. The name for this new model was entirely apt – the Classic.

Launched at the 1992 Birmingham Motor Show, the new Classic really was like a time-warp from the 1960s in its specification. As much can be concluded from what it did *not* have. It had no carpets, no rev-counter, no fuel gauge, no spare wheel, no heater, no weather equipment and not even a windscreen. There were instead two Brooklands aero screens to deflect air over the passengers' heads.

The rest of the specification was equally basic. The engine was the 1600GT crossflow unit with a single downdraught carburettor and 84bhp, as first seen way back in 1968. The wheels were plain steel and the seat was a basic bench affair. Compared to the GTS, the Classic was £1,500 cheaper (with a sensational retail price of just £7,450).

At that price the Classic attracted a lot of custom into the showroom. But the basic specification was very hard to live with day-to-day – the lack of a windscreen especially so. Therefore Caterham offered an 'SE' (Special

A pared-down specification hardly diluted the fun factor, although the lack of a windscreen severely limited the car's all-round usability, and most buyers opted to fit a full screen.

Most Classics were in fact sold with an SE package included, returning the full windscreen, weather gear and instruments.

Equipment) package that added back in the screen, weather gear, instruments, carpets and alloy wheels (including a spare). You also had the Sprint-spec engine with its twin Weber sidedraught carbs and 100bhp (which could also be ordered as an extra with the base Classic). It was a curious fact that more than 100 examples of the Classic SE were sold before a single basic Classic left the factory.

The Classic was a very popular model, representing a live-axle entry-level 7 for an enticingly low price. Towards the end of its life, it was also offered with the 135bhp Supersprint engine as an option. Ultimately the exhaustion of Ford crossflow engine supplies (they had been imported from South Africa) forced Caterham to look elsewhere for its entry-level engine – to Vauxhall in fact. The Ford crossflow Classic did remain available without an engine thereafter.

Specification	
Engine	Ford 1600GT (Sprint or 1700 Supersprint optional)
Capacity	1,598cc
Bore x stroke	80.96 x 77.62mm
Induction	Single Weber carburettor
Compression ratio	9.0:1
Max power	84bhp (63kW) at 5,500rpm
Max torque	91lb ft (123Nm) at 3,500rpm
Gearbox	Ford four-speed (five-speed or six-speed optional)
Brakes	Girling 9in front discs, 8in rear drums
Steering	Rack-and-pinion
Weight	1,200lb (625kg)
Top speed	104mph (167kph)
0-60mph	7.7sec
50-70mph in top	6.7sec
Number produced	N/A

1.4 K-series
Rover power adds new sparkle

With Rover K-series power, the 7 entered a new generation. The lightweight, all-alloy, twin cam and all-British engine was perfect for the 7.

Summary

Rover's brand-new K-series engine powers the 7 in the heartland of the range – sweet-revving, lightweight and reliable, it overcame initial resistance to its low 1.4 litres capacity and 110bhp power output.

Identifying features

Alloy-cased five-speed gearbox (six-speed optional), de Dion rear axle, 'Caterham K-series' branded engine, chassis numbers within sequence 5538–20616 and with RI chassis code.

Since the earliest days of the Lotus 7, the sports car icon had always been associated with engines from one source above all – Ford. That changed dramatically when, in the greatest sea change yet in the 7's life at Caterham, a new engine supplier was chosen. When work started in 1990, the switch from Ford engines to the Rover K-series represented the first change of engine block since 1961! But this was perhaps not such a huge revolution as might be imagined, for there was a precedent as a Rover Group powerplant (the BMC A-series engine) had been used in very early Lotus 7s.

Taken from the new Rover Metro GTI – launched at the same time as the new Caterham – the 1.4-litre K-series engine was in many ways an inspired choice. 'Rover seemed to have designed an engine especially for the 7', commented Caterham's Jez Coates.

First, it was very light (being an all-alloy unit), it had 16 valves, twin overhead camshafts and excellent emissions performance. It was a reasonably powerful engine; in fuel-injected guise it developed 110bhp at 6,000rpm. An all-new exhaust system was created for the K-series, initially rear-exit but later changed to a side-exit because the engine bay catalytic converter installation was so complex. A catalyst had been optional from the start but became mandatory from January 1993 when new legislation demanded, and it was then positioned within the side-mounted exhaust.

The fuel-injected K-series engine was in many ways ideal. Even though in its original form it only had 1.4 litres and 110bhp, it proved very flexible.

Specification	
Engine	Rover K-series
Capacity	1,397cc
Bore x stroke	75 x 79mm
Induction	Rover multi-point fuel injection
Compression ratio	10.5:1
Max power	110bhp (82kW) at 6,000rpm (103bhp (77kW) with catalyst)
Max torque	96lb ft at 5,000rpm (94lb ft (127Nm) with catalyst)
Gearbox	Ford Sierra five-speed or Caterham six-speed
Brakes	9in (228mm) discs front and rear
Steering	Rack-and-pinion
Weight	1,200lb (545kg)
Top speed	103mph (166kph)
0-60mph	6.8sec
50-70mph in 4th	7.9sec
Number produced	N/A

The catalyst dropped the overall power by 7bhp.

In the 7 the K-series powerplant had to be rotated by 90 degrees so that it could be mounted longitudinally, and was also inclined at a 15-degree angle in order for the multipoint fuel injection system to fit. Carburettors had been considered but it was felt that changing legislation dictated the use of Rover multipoint fuel injection.

The underpinnings were also significantly changed. The chassis had to be slightly modified, with the upper engine bay diagonals spread out by an inch at the rear, leading to a narrowing of the pedal box. The five-speed Ford gearbox was retained but was now encased in a specially cast light alloy bell housing, and there was a lighter radiator too. Altogether the engine/gearbox installation was some 35kg less than the Ford pushrod set-up, which definitely helped the 7's handling balance.

In raw figures, the new K-series performed at least as well as the Sprint-engined 7, with a claimed 6.7-second 0–60mph time and a top speed of 112mph. But it was more the subjective elements of the drive that proved truly convincing and, as chief engineer Jez Coates put it, this was 'the most 7-like 7 we've produced.' *Autocar* magazine certainly agreed when it called the new car 'arguably the most enjoyable car Caterham makes.'

The 1.4-litre engine lacked flexibility in the lower rev bands, but it delighted in a full use of revs, and was especially sweet and strong-performing above 4,000rpm. Throttle response was also excellent. Perhaps the biggest criticism of the K-series was the mismatch of the Ford's five-speed ratios with the torque spread, blunting otherwise sparkling performance, which prompted the

Rover launched its Metro GTi at the same time as the 7 K-series, emphasising the close links between Rover and Caterham. The engine was turned longitudinally in the 7 but remained tilted at a 15-degree angle to fit the 7's engine bay.

development of Caterham's own six-speed gearbox to suit the Rover engine.

The lighter drivetrain weight benefited steering response and lightness to a significant degree. Highly informative, it enabled previously unvisited heights of handling adjustability via the throttle and wheel. Neutral four-wheel drifts were not only possible but delightfully easy to sustain.

When launched at London's Docklands in July 1991, the K-series cost £13,883 in kit form. This was regarded at the time as quite expensive, as it was about the same price as a Supersprint, which had more power (135bhp) and a larger capacity (1,700cc). Whatever is said about efficiency and light weight, some customers always want a certain minimum cubic centimetrage, and 1,400cc was regarded as insufficient by some customers. However, after initial resistance, buyers embraced the new Rover engine choice by degrees. This was accepted as perhaps the sweetest of all the engine options yet fitted to a 7, although it took the more powerful 1.4 Supersport engine to swing the balance definitively in favour of the K-series in customers' minds. By 1994, the K-series was the most popular Caterham engine installation, and the 1.4 engine paved the way for larger, 1.6 and 1.8-litre versions of this unit. The last roadgoing non-Supersport 1.4-litre Caterham was built in 1996.

Sweet-running, flexible and willing, the K-series engine – even in 1.4-litre form – provided perhaps the most satisfying drive of any then-current Caterham; 0–60mph took 6.8 seconds.

The K-series became the most popular engine choice for factory-built 7s in the mid to late 1990s, gaining widespread acceptance.

1.4 K-series Supersport

Boosted power creates special 'K'

The Rover K-series engine's 110bhp was clearly not enough to tempt customers away from the 135bhp Supersprint, which cost about the same to buy as the K-series 7, but which was rapidly becoming 'yesterday's motor'. Several options were considered for boosting the Rover's power output, including turbocharging, supercharging and revised pistons and porting, but all were rejected as too costly.

Caterham then approached Rover, asking for a 1.4-litre K-series to be modified to produce a target of 100bhp per litre. Rover could not sanction such a project officially but six Rover employees formed a 'Saturday Morning Club' to do the work required in their spare time.

Work on the engine consisted of fitting the reprofiled camshafts from the Project Pride Metro record-breaker, a new larger-bore free-flow inlet manifold and plenum chamber, plus a specially mapped Motorola ECU allowing the engine to rev to a much higher red line (up to 7,600rpm). The capacity was left untouched at 1,397cc but the power output rose from 110bhp to 128bhp – not far off Caterham's ideal 100bhp per litre target and virtually the same power output as the Supersprint engine.

One novel fringe benefit of the new ECU was the fact that it had software for an air conditioning system, which for obvious reasons was entirely redundant on a Caterham. So the software was rewritten to activate a light

The 1.4 Supersport got some of the urge that the standard K-series lacked, with a 0–60mph in 6.0 seconds dead, and a greater ability to exploit the balance of the chassis.

Summary

Rover's 'Saturday Morning Club' provides the K-series engine with an extra 25bhp and the credibility to oust the Ford Supersprint engine at last.

Identifying features

Tuned 'Caterham K-series' branded engine, alloy-cased five-speed gearbox (six-speed optional), de Dion rear axle, dash-mounted gearchange light, RI chassis code.

on the dashboard whenever the revs reached 7,400rpm. This gearchange indicator had obvious parallels with the world of British Touring Cars and Formula 1, which was no bad thing.

The new engine was acclaimed in road tests and was ideally matched to the Caterham six-speed gearbox, and *Performance Car* said, 'the extra urge doesn't corrupt the essential intimacy and accessibility of the car. If anything, it makes it easier to exploit.'

The tuned K-series model was branded the Supersport and it turned the corner as far as the K-series engine was concerned. It was finally a genuine alternative to the more powerful Supersprint engine. The 1.4-litre Supersport engine lasted until 1996, when the new 1.6-litre K-series engine took over. For 1996 there was a limited run of 1.4-litre Road-Sport 7s (covered separately), although the 1.4-litre Supersport engine did actually survive a little longer in racing 7s.

Specification	
Engine	Rover K-series Supersport
Capacity	1,397cc
Bore x stroke	75 x 79mm
Induction	Rover multi-point fuel injection
Compression ratio	10.0:1
Max power	128bhp (95kW) at 7,400rpm
Max torque	100lb ft (136Nm) at 5,000rpm
Gearbox	Ford Sierra V6 five-speed or Caterham six-speed
Brakes	9in discs front and rear
Steering	Rack-and-pinion
Weight	1,200lb (544kg)
Top speed	114mph (183kph)
0-60mph	6.0sec
50-70mph in 4th	4.8sec
Number produced	N/A

A 'Supersport' casting identified the new engine, which gained reprofiled camshafts, a large-bore free-flow inlet manifold and a specially mapped ECU.

Road-Sport

Lightweight special edition is a 'junior JPE'

A 'junior JPE' is what *Autocar* called the Road-Sport when it was launched in January 1996. That is perhaps stretching the point, but the limited production Road-Sport did incorporate some of the JPE's weight-saving measures in its delectable specification.

In truth this was a run-out special edition to mark the end of the road for the 1.4-litre K-series engine, for 1996 saw the introduction of the 1.6-litre K-series as the new mid-range Caterham engine, the reasoning being the larger engine had greater commercial appeal.

The Road-Sport enjoyed the new, 1996 chassis with its stiffer construction, revised suspension and its handbrake resited centrally on the transmission tunnel. Its engine was the 1.4-litre K-series Supersport unit with 128bhp on tap and the transmission was Caterham's branded six-speed close-ratio unit, which had garnered such huge praise from the motoring press. In all other respects under the skin, the Road-Sport duplicated the specification of the 1.4 Supersport.

The JPE-derived weight-savers were the carbon fibre front cycle wings and carbon fibre rear wing protectors, which were left in an unpainted finish that looked just right and shaved probably 15kg off the weight of a standard Supersport-engined 7. The Road-Sport enjoyed several other unique features, including an anthracite-finish set of Minilite-style 14-inch alloy wheels that matched the carbon fibre wings, a special metallic paint finish in either yellow or green, a black grille and black windscreen surround, lightweight leather-trimmed seats, a Momo steering wheel, painted roll-over bar, special decals and a dashboard-mounted plaque. Also thrown in were a personalised jacket and a free driver training day.

Only 30 Road-Sports were built, at a cost of £16,995 in component form or £20,155 fully built. It was also possible for owners to upgrade their Road-Sport to racing specification (which presumably ought to be called the Race-Sport). This limited edition has become a real collector's item among 7 enthusiasts but the rarity of this model means that examples very seldom come up for sale.

The Road-Sport offered lots of goodies, including carbon fibre components and anthracite-finish alloy wheels, for a bargain price.

Summary

Strictly limited-production 1.4 Supersport run-out edition with an enticing specification of JPE lightweight wings, leather trim, special paint and wheels and a six-speed gearbox.

Identifying features

1.4 Supersport engine, six-speed gearbox, carbon fibre front wings, anthracite 14-inch alloy wheels, metallic paint, black grille and windscreen, leather seats, decals, dash plaque, chassis numbers within sequence 20092–20117.

Specification

Engine	Rover K-series Supersport
Capacity	1,397cc
Bore x stroke	75 x 79mm
Induction	Rover multi-point fuel injection
Compression ratio	10.0:1
Max power	128bhp (95kW) at 7,400rpm
Max torque	100lb ft (136Nm) at 5,000rpm
Gearbox	Caterham six-speed
Brakes	9in discs front and rear
Steering	Rack-and-pinion
Weight	1,166lb (529kg)
Top speed	114mph (183kph)
0-60mph	6.0sec
50-70mph in 4th	4.8sec
Number produced	30

Caterham 7 Road-Sport (1996)

JPE

Jonatham Palmer endorses the ultimate 7

Ex-F1 racer Dr Jonathan Palmer helped with the development of the spectacular JPE and lent it its name: Jonathan Palmer Evolution.

Summary

Super-lightweight, super-powerful, highly developed JPE has Jonathan Palmer endorsement and one of the most explosive drives of any car on the planet.

Identifying features

Weber Alpha-equipped SRE engine, yellow cam cover, Dymag magnesium wheels, JPE badging, Quaife gearbox, vented discs and four-pot callipers, chassis numbers within sequence 5785–30658 with 'JPE' or 'VXRME' chassis code.

Many Caterhams have achieved an exalted status: the original Twin Cam, the HPC and the Superlight to name but three. But none matches the incomparable JPE, an absolute and extreme icon of technical achievement, extravagant specification and ultra-light weight. It remains perhaps the pinnacle of the light weight/high power imperative.

The mighty JPE was the first-ever cost-no-object 7 conceived at Caterham. As much can be gathered from the cost of the engine alone – estimated at £13,000. Of course, this was a very special engine, and a very special car. The JPE was intended as a project with the ultimate specification, an end-of-an-era celebration before emissions laws finally banished 'dirty' monsters to the wilderness.

Swindon Racing Engines (SRE) supplied Caterham with a version of the Vauxhall 2.0-litre engine that virtually matched British Touring Car Championship specifications. It had Weber Alpha fuel injection for the sake of driveability but still churned out 250bhp at a screaming 7,750rpm on a very high 12.0:1 compression ratio.

The JPE was designed to be an ultra-lightweight machine. To get down to just 530kg (1,168lb), it swapped a windscreen for a Perspex wind deflector, had carbon fibre wings instead of glassfibre, had no roof, heater, spare or even paint and boasted specially made carbon fibre seats. This delivered a

Central to the JPE was its Vauxhall twin-cam-based engine. Developed by Swindon Racing Engines, it was virtually to the same specification as that of the Vauxhall BTCC racing team.

Specification	
Engine	SRE-modified Vauxhall twin cam
Capacity	1,998cc (last cars were 2.1 or 2.2 litres)
Bore x stroke	86 x 86mm
Induction	Weber Alpha electronic fuel injection
Compression ratio	12.0:1
Max power	250bhp (186kW) at 7,750rpm
Max torque	186lb ft (252Nm) at 6,250rpm
Gearbox	Quaife straight-cut five-speed
Brakes	10in ventilated front discs, 9in solid rear discs
Steering	Caterham rack-and-pinion
Weight	1,168lb (530kg)
Top speed	150mph (241kph)
0-60mph	3.46sec
50-70mph in top	6.0sec
Number produced	53

Thanks to its favourable gearing, the JPE was a phenomenal 0–60mph tool, taking the world record at 3.46 seconds. It is seen here taking the record for accelerating to 100mph and braking back to zero, a feat Jonathan Palmer performed in just 12.6 seconds.

Caterham

7 JPE (1992–2001)

power-to-weight ratio of 472bhp per tonne.

The rest of the spec followed suit. An aluminium saddle fuel tank was positioned above the rear axle, there was a lightweight aluminium radiator, a Quaife straight-cut close-ratio five-speed gearbox, matched exhaust system, aluminium-cased steering rack, four-piston alloy front callipers and ventilated discs. Caterham specified very lightweight Dymag magnesium wheels (6.5 x 15-inch front, 7.5 x 15-inch rear), shod with 205 front and 225 rear Yokohama A-008R tyres.

The JPE tag stood for Jonathan Palmer Evolution, after the ex-Formula 1 racer and then-current McLaren F1 test driver became involved in testing the car. He commented: 'It's the nearest thing to a Formula 1 car on the road . . . It's a difficult car to drive on the limit, but that's the whole challenge. The engine is very peaky; the power only really comes on strongly at 6,500rpm but it's also very docile lower down.'

The JPE was the most expensive Caterham ever produced, with an ultra-light specification that read like a wish-list for hardened 7 enthusiasts. Road testers were blown away – almost literally – by the sheer pace and stopping power of the latest Caterham. Not all JPEs were fluorescent yellow, as this black car (below) on test with *Autocar* magazine proves.

Inside the cockpit, there were six-point racing harnesses plus a personalised helmet and steering wheel. Controversy surrounded the original instrument pack, which had a speedo with no markings above 70mph and a rev counter with almost no markings at all. Ultimately the rev counter eschewed a red line for a green band between 6,500rpm and 8,200rpm to indicate where you should be most of the time, and the speedo was marked to 150mph. Because of its improved aerodynamic performance, the JPE was a genuine 150mph car.

Huge publicity always surrounded the JPE. For a start, it briefly made it into the *Guinness Book of World Records* with an amazing 3.46-second 0-60mph time, achieved by *Fast Lane* magazine. *Autocar & Motor* ran a story in which the JPE performed the 0–100–0mph sprint-and-stop time of 12.6 seconds with Jonathan Palmer at the wheel – over three seconds faster than a Ferrari F40. The magazine called the JPE 'unequivocally the world's fastest-accelerating production car.'

Road testers rained praise down on the JPE's phenomenal power surge, extraordinary brakes, sharp gearchange and tenacious grip. The response of the engine was the JPE's most memorable feature. Below 5,500rpm it felt like it was just clearing its throat, while the fireworks really started above 6,500rpm (marked by that green line), right up to its rev limiter at

8,200rpm. This was quite a beast, something you got as much out of as you put in.

The gear ratios were ideally placed to keep the surge of power flowing as the JPE rocketed forward on a mission to warp reality. Traction was surprisingly good and the tyres gripped with tenacity. The chassis always felt perfectly capable of handling that explosive power. And the brakes were possibly the best of any road car then available.

No-one who drove the JPE could ignore the ear-splitting noise of the engine: as *Car* magazine put it: 'The engine pops and grunts and babbles, its bad attitude ripping to shreds the veneer of sophistication the engine management tries to impart.' No less loud was the paint scheme. The first JPE was famously painted in fluorescent yellow, with matching yellow six-point harnesses, wheels, cam cover, exhaust guard inserts, instruments and roll-over bar. (Ironically, paint was actually an option on the JPE as an unpainted finish saved 2kg in overall weight!) Yellow was not the only colour in which the JPE was supplied to buyers, however, and there were many willing customers for this astronomically priced, £34,950 projectile, although by far the majority were exported to Japan.

Ultimately, the JPE was phased out after ten years because engines were becoming difficult to source from Vauxhall, it was an expensive car to manufacture and the Superlight R500 had become the natural successor. Some of the last ten cars had 2.1 or 2.2-litre SRE engines with roller barrels and even more power. The final JPE was in build in 2001, a very special car with a 290bhp SRE powerplant, twin roller barrels with carbon trumpets, a one-off wiring loom and engine management system, and a special carbon fibre dash.

With its cut-down screen, hard-edged and peaky engine and ultra-sharp dynamics, the JPE was at once the most rewarding and challenging Caterham yet constructed.

The interior gained carbon fibre seats, special harnesses and controversial gauges.

97

S7 Competition R

Swiss market powerhouse packs over 300bhp

Caterham's Swiss agent, Kumschick Cars, sold the extraordinary Opel 2.0 Turbo powered S7 Competition R. Note the very wide wheels and the extra vents in the nose cone.

Summary

Someone had to make a turbocharged 7 and the Swiss Caterham importer did it in no mean measure, as this fearsome 300bhp beast proves.

Identifying features

Turbocharged GM 2.0 twin cam engine, special alloy wheels, vaned nose cone, under-wing aerodynamic aids, limited slip diff, six-speed gearbox, race brakes/clutch, chassis numbers within sequence 3281–21886.

Export and foreign-market 7s have often had unique quirks, but one such car stands out above the rest with a specification that eclipses all other export models. The S7 Competition R is, in short, the most ballistically manic and easily the most expensive official 7 ever produced.

It was an exclusive development of Fredy Kumschick, the Swiss Caterham importer. While in Britain, Caterham chose not to pursue an experiment it began with a turbocharged Vauxhall HPC prototype, Kumschick did precisely that.

The engine was a highly developed Vauxhall/Opel 2.0-litre twin-cam Rallye unit with KKK turbocharging. The result was no less than 300bhp at 6,500rpm and 296lb ft of torque at 5,200rpm – and later development increased this to 320bhp and 320lb ft! This translated to a top speed of 156mph and a 0–100kph time of 3.4 seconds. Driving this beast required huge skill, not to say restraint on public roads – and this was an entirely road-legal car, although most owners used theirs mainly on the track, of course.

Other special features of the Competition R included dry-sump lubrication, racing brake discs and clutch, ABS, an AP Suretrac limited slip differential, Koni F1 dampers and aluminium for the radiator, oil cooler and intercooler. Caterham's six-speed gearbox was the natural transmission choice.

Externally the Competition R benefited from massive 8 x 16-inch front and 9 x 16-inch rear alloy wheels with 205/55 ZR16 front and 225/50 ZR16 Pirelli Zero C tyres. Both front and rear wings had extra aerodynamic appendages underneath them and the nose cone incorporated twin cooling vanes on the upper surface.

Available exclusively for personal registration in Switzerland in left-hand drive only, the S7 Competition R carried a brain-numbing price tag of 116,000 (later 128,000) Swiss francs (equating to £65,000, or twice the cost of a Superlight R500). Even at this price it did find customers – some 25 have been sold following its launch at the Geneva Motor Show, and it has since made regular appearances at this event. The very last car (for Mr Kumschick) had no less than 330bhp on tap and weighed only 555kg . . .

Specification	
Engine	Vauxhall/Opel Rallye twin-cam turbo
Capacity	1,998cc
Bore x stroke	86 x 86mm
Induction	Fuel injection
Compression ratio	9.1:1
Max power	300bhp (223kW) at 6,500rpm (later 320bhp (238kW))
Max torque	296lb ft (402Nm) at 5,200rpm (later 320lb ft (434Nm))
Gearbox	Caterham six-speed
Brakes	Racing ventilated discs, 10.4in front, 10.1in rear
Steering	Rack-and-pinion
Weight	1,278lb (580kg)
Top speed	156mph (251kph)
0-60mph	3.3sec
50-70mph in top	N/A
Number produced	25

The Opel twin cam turbo powerplant was a tight squeeze, but was a beautifully engineered installation. At 300bhp, it was the most ferocious engine ever fitted to an official Caterham model.

Kumschick regularly displayed at the Geneva Motor Show, lending extra credibility to the ferocious Competition R model.

1.6 K-series/
Supersport/Roadsport
1.6-litre power from Rover

Now that the 1.6-litre K-series engine was available, the 7 became more tractable, a better performer and gained greater acceptance with the buying public.

Summary

Larger-capacity K-series engine has more power and torque and comes in a much-modified chassis with superior ride quality.

Identifying features

1.6-litre Caterham-branded Rover engine, built-in immobiliser, central handbrake lever, Caterham-branded instruments, first chassis number 6391.

Caterham's special relationship with Rover led it to trial-fit larger K-series engines in the 7 as early as 1993. Why then did Caterham opt for the 1.6-litre unit to replace the 1.4 when it could have gone straight for the MGF's 1.8-litre powerplant? Principally, Rover could only supply the smaller engine to start with. Additionally, the shorter-stroke crank of the 1600 made it sweeter than the 1800, while it was more refined, less expensive and the future Supersport modifications would produce almost as much power as the projected 1800 Supersport unit.

So it was that, after an October 1995 Motor Show debut, the standard K-series chosen in 1996 was the 1.6-litre, as fitted to the Rover 200. It had more power than the 1.4-litre (115bhp at 6,000rpm compared to 103bhp at 6,000rpm), more torque and of course the added kudos of extra cubic inches. There was a new fuel injection system, Rover's MEMS set-up that incorporated a computerised engine immobiliser with the ECU.

The 1996 Caterham also underwent some significant chassis changes which greatly improved overall driveability. Because of substantial tunnel tubework and stressed panelling, it was 30 per cent stiffer and the roll-over bar now sat one inch taller and sloped forwards. Also, the handbrake was moved from its traditional and very awkward passenger footwell location to the centre tunnel, removing the last remaining component that had not

The 1.6-litre K-series quickly acquired the mantle of the most popular engine among cars built at the factory. The model name was changed to Roadsport in 1999.

changed since the days of the Lotus 7.

But perhaps the most telling change was in the suspension department. Following a long development process with Bilstein, the dampers were revalved and lengthened, and Caterham specified revised anti-roll bar settings, increased roll-on camber and new anti-dive geometry. For the first time, progressive rate rear springs were fitted to compensate for the larger variations in rear axle loading. These suspension alterations were not about handling, which was adjudged to be difficult to improve, but were geared towards improving composure on bumpy surfaces where the stiffly sprung 7 could easily be thrown off line. In some sections of the press this was regarded as 'softening' the 7's appeal, although this verdict is perhaps unfair; the extra compliance made the 7 a much more complete car without affecting its handling balance. It was just that the press liked its 7s to be raw and 'real' – a soft ride was not what the 7 was about, said some. To combat the criticism, a Supersport suspension package was offered, adding an adjustable rear anti-roll bar and a thicker front bar, a version that *Performance Car*'s John Barker was happy to endorse.

As before, there was a Supersport version of the K-series, available as a £998 option. This was developed by Rover exclusively for Caterham. Engine management control and uprated camshafts provided high-revving extra power – now rated at 138bhp at 7,000rpm (10bhp more than the 1.4 Supersport); this figure was later revised to 133bhp to reflect its genuine output with catalytic converter in place. As before, there was a Supersport gearchange warning light that came on at 7,400rpm, 200rpm below the rev limiter.

Road testers were in no doubt that the new engine provided far greater torque and flexibility than the 1.4 engine. It picked up more cleanly from low revs, yet retained the blistering pace and razor-sharp throttle response at high revs. In combination with the ultra-close six-speed gearbox, the new drivetrain provided hugely impressive in-gear acceleration times, with only 800rpm lost in each of the first five gears. And the noise remained every bit as nerve-stimulating.

In 1999, the whole K-series Caterham range was rebadged as the Roadsport to reflect its role as the all-round 7 for road and everyday use. The 1.6-litre engine became instantly the most popular engine choice for factory-built 7s, representing one in every three sales in 2001, for example.

At the 2000 Birmingham Motor Show, a new T-Type interior trim package was displayed as an update of the S-Type trim, but the general movement was towards lighter weight in 7s and the lack of interest in the package meant that it was never produced; indeed, even the S-Type package was removed from the price lists the following year.

The 1.6 engine was available in 115bhp standard and (as pictured) 133bhp Supersport forms. The Supersport ECU allowed for gear change lights to be wired in on the dashboard.

Specification	
Engine	Rover K-series/Supersport
Capacity	1,588cc
Bore x stroke	80 x 79mm
Induction	Rover multi-point fuel injection
Compression ratio	10.5:1
Max power	115bhp (86kW) at 6,000rpm/133bhp (99kW) at 7,000rpm
Max torque	107lb ft (145Nm) at 3,000rpm/110lb ft (149Nm) at 5,000rpm
Gearbox	Ford Sierra V6 five-speed or Caterham six-speed
Brakes	9in (228mm) discs front and rear
Steering	Rack-and-pinion
Weight	1,200lb (544kg)
Top speed	108mph/112mph (174kph/180kph)
0–60mph	6.2/6.0sec
50–70mph in 4th	N/A/4.7sec
Number produced	Still in production

40th Anniversary

Still young at 40 years

Forty years of the 7 were celebrated in 1997 with the arrival of another anniversary edition, with its special paint, 'Prisoner' wheels, half-S-Type leather trim, lightweight seats and a numbered plaque.

Very few cars make it to 40 years old and to the author's knowledge, the 7 was the first car ever to celebrate with a 40th Anniversary special edition. In fact the celebratory model was first displayed at the October 1996 Birmingham Motor Show, 39 years after the first motor show appearance of the Lotus 7 Series 1, although deliveries began in 1997.

The new special edition very much followed in the footsteps of the 35th Anniversary model in terms of its up-market specification. There was a brand-new paint scheme, consisting of pearlescent ruby main body colour with a silver bonnet stripe and black coachlining. The silver extended down to envelope the maw of the nose cone and the grille incorporated the '7' logo. Like the 35th, Prisoner-style 15-inch alloy wheels were once again fitted as standard

Inside, the Anniversary was trimmed in Half-S-Type leather trim (usually an £807 option), with full S-Type trim costing an extra £998. In both cases the new, 1996 lightweight seats were fitted, half the weight of the previous seats. There was also a standard Motolita steering wheel, or a Racetech item as a no-cost option (allowing the possibility of a quick-release system). To mark the 40th Anniversary, a special, numbered plaque accompanied each car on its dashboard, which attested to its authenticity.

The base price was £15,950 in kit form for a 1.6 K-series powered

Summary

Another birthday 7 with an up-market specification and a unique red-and-silver paint scheme – making it a sought-after model.

Identifying features

Pearlescent red-and-silver paint, dashboard plaque, half-leather trim, Prisoner alloys, chassis numbers within sequence 20427–20845.

example. Other engine options included the 1.6 Supersport (£998 extra) or the 2.0 Vauxhall engine (£3,500 extra), the latter in carburettor form only (and one of the last 7s to have carbs rather than injection). Nearly £20,000 for the Vauxhall-engined 40th Anniversary made it one of the most expensive 7s yet produced, but then there were up to £1,600 worth of extras for not much more than the standard cars' prices. The 40th Anniversary model was still on the price lists at the 1998 Geneva Motor Show and it remains a very sought-after model in enthusiast circles.

Specification	
Engine	Rover K-series (or Supersport or Vauxhall carb)
Capacity	1,588cc
Bore x stroke	80 x 79mm
Induction	Rover multi-point fuel injection
Compression ratio	10.5:1
Max power	115bhp (86kW) at 6,000rpm
Max torque	107lb ft (145Nm) at 3,000rpm
Gearbox	Ford Sierra five-speed or Caterham six-speed
Brakes	9in discs front and rear
Steering	Rack-and-pinion
Weight	1,200lb (544kg)
Top speed	108mph (174kph)
0-60mph	6.2sec
50-70mph in 4th	N/A/4.7sec
Number produced	67

The unique 40th Anniversary paint scheme consisted of deep red paint with a lined silver stripe down the bonnet and on to the nose cone.

Superlight 1.6
Adding lightness invents a new icon

The idea for the Superlight was inspired: take a variety of lightweight parts already developed by Caterham for the JPE and create a very light 7 with a 1.6-litre Supersport engine.

Summary

Lightest-yet Caterham has chassis mods and a stripped-out spec to turn it into a paragon for the acceleration junkie or motorsports-minded owner.

Identifying features

Carbon fibre wings, nose cone, dash and mirrors, wind deflector, glassfibre seats, ventilated front discs, limited-slip differential, six-speed gearbox, numbered dash plaque, first chassis number 30146. Note that cars were built to order and individual specs differ (e.g. windscreens are common fitments).

Alongside the 40th Anniversary model at the 1996 Birmingham Motor Show debuted an even more exciting model – and highly significant because it launched the Superlight badge to the world. It was a stark rebuff to the critics who had described the latest 1996 chassis as 'soft' and a strong reply to pundits who had placed the new Lotus Elise above the Caterham as a fun machine.

In its philosophy of 'adding lightness', the Superlight was the perfect expression of Colin Chapman's original ideals. With its all-up weight of only 468kg (1,031lb), it was the lightest 7 yet produced by Caterham. Costing £17,495 (£455 more than the 1.6 Supersport), it was touted as being 'for the enthusiast wanting a lighter car for circuit use, hill-climbing, sprinting or simply a dynamic 7 for the road.'

Interestingly, it was created almost entirely using parts that were already available for the 7. So it got the existing Supersport K-series engine, JPE-type wind deflector and carbon fibre panels and composite seats, for example.

This was a very focused new 7 – to build the lightest car possible. Like the JPE, it did without heavy items of equipment such as weather equipment, carpets, wing protectors, spare wheel and heater and the windscreen was replaced by a JPE-style black wind deflector. The cycle wings and nose cone

Weighing only 468kg, the 133bhp Superlight was a very sharp performer, and was also reasonably priced. Small wonder the Superlight brand became an instant hit.

Specification

Engine	Rover K-series Supersport (other engines available)
Capacity	1,588cc
Bore x stroke	80 x 79mm
Induction	Rover multi-point fuel injection
Compression ratio	10.5:1
Max power	133bhp (99kW) at 7,000rpm
Max torque	110lb ft (149Nm) at 5,000rpm
Gearbox	Caterham six-speed
Brakes	10in ventilated front discs, 9in solid rear discs
Steering	Rack-and-pinion
Weight	1,031lb (468kg)
Top speed	129mph (208kph)
0-60mph	4.7sec
30-70mph	4.5sec
Number produced	176 to date

Special decals and a plaque identified genuine Caterham Superlight models.

With a 0–60mph time of just 4.7 seconds, this was one of the quickest 7s ever.

were in lightweight carbon fibre and a stripped-out interior featured composite race seats, four-point racing harnesses and carbon fibre for the dash and rear-view mirrors. The Superlight even came in an unpainted finish to save an extra two kilograms! Options were listed according to their impact on weight – all of them adding weight, with the exception of Kevlar seats, which saved 3.2 kilograms.

The suspension settings reverted to the stiffer Supersport package and reinstated an adjustable rear anti-roll bar. The Superlight became the first 7 to adopt the new, wide-track front suspension (now matching the rear track at 1,336mm, some 66mm wider than the standard front suspension). This made it highly communicative for the enthusiastic driver. Even more so with the Formula Ford Avon intermediate crossply tyres on the 13-inch alloys – very grippy in the dry, a bit of a handful in the wet but all completely road legal and e-marked. Part of the reason they were chosen was because they were so lightweight.

The standard Superlight engine was the 1.6 Supersport with its easily accessible 133bhp and a competition exhaust. That equated to a power-to-weight ratio of 283bhp per tonne, translating the Superlight into the fastest-accelerating 7 of the lot, shy only of the JPE. It was hard to believe, but the 1.6 Superlight was even quicker through the gears than a 175bhp Vauxhall-engined HPC. The standard Caterham six-speed close-ratio gearbox certainly helped, as did the AP single-plate racing clutch and limited slip differential. Another highlight was ventilated 10-inch front discs with four-pot callipers. Other engines were available if you wished, principally the 1.8 Supersport and even the 1.8 VVC.

This was one car where the whole definitely exceeded sum of the parts. It was highly praised in the motoring press for its focused approach to dynamics. This was the beginning of Caterham's move towards a more focused driving experience with the emphasis on light weight at the expense of all creature comforts. Crucially, it raised the 7 to new heights of performance and handling that the Lotus Elise could not match. Some road testers believe the Superlight to be still the best car Caterham builds today.

Superlight R

R is for Racer

Stick a Rover/Caterham VHPD engine in the Superlight and you get a Superlight R, a truly ferocious road machine. It was perhaps better suited as a track day car for the experienced enthusiast.

Summary

Utterly explosive performance from the VHPD engine makes the ultra-lightweight 'R' version of the Superlight almost too hot to handle.

Identifying features

VHPD engine, carbon fibre wings, nose cone, dash and mirrors, wind deflector, glassfibre seats, ventilated front discs, limited-slip differential, six-speed gearbox, numbered dash plaque, first chassis number 20538 (car number 1 has chassis number 20873)

What a difference the addition of one simple 'R' makes to the Superlight concept. While the 'ordinary' Superlight was devilishly fast and very focussed, the 'R' exploded the 7's performance envelope to extraordinary new highs.

Central to the new car was its VHPD (Very High Performance Derivative) engine, conceived by Rover in conjunction with Caterham. For Rover's part, it would be the engine for the Rover 200 single-make series, while for Caterham it was the unit that would replace the Vauxhall racer. Caterham's main criterion was that it had to reach 190bhp to match the Vauxhall racer's output. The roadgoing project followed on, and was broadly remarkably similar to the racer.

The cracking VHPD powerplant was based on the MGF's 1.8-litre engine. Numerous modifications were wrought on the K-series engine, including a nitro-carburised crankshaft, forged pistons, enlarged-port cylinder head, bigger inlet and exhaust valves, high-lift/duration camshafts, bespoke inlet manifold and throttle fuel body injection and a specially mapped Rover MEMS 1.9 engine management system.

This very special engine delivered its 190bhp at 7,500rpm with a maximum rev limit of 8,000rpm and a Supersport-type gearchange warning light higher up the rev band at 7,750rpm. Performance was in new territory

Specification	
Engine	Caterham Motorsport/ Rover K-series VHPD
Capacity	1,796cc
Bore x stroke	80 x 89.3mm
Induction	Rover multi-point fuel injection
Compression ratio	10.5:1
Max power	190bhp (142kW) at 7,500rpm (race version 200bhp (149kW))
Max torque	150lb ft (203Nm) at 5,750rpm
Gearbox	Caterham six-speed
Brakes	10in ventilated front discs, 9in solid rear discs
Steering	Rack-and-pinion
Weight	1,080lb (490kg)
Top speed	140mph (225kph)
0-60mph	4.0sec
50-70mph	N/A
Number produced	110 to date

The 'R' boasted race-spec items like limited slip differential, ventilated front discs with four-pot alloy front callipers and quick-release steering wheel, plus a sharper chassis and race-spec 13-inch two-piece split-rim alloy wheels.

(for anything less than a JPE, at any rate). You would expect no less from a car with over 400bhp per tonne; 0–100mph came up, shatteringly, in under nine seconds. Small wonder an 'R' took the Nürburgring lap record for production cars at just over eight minutes. And the race version with its roller barrels developed an extra 10bhp. . . .

Like the Superlight, the 'R' gained many race-specification features, such as AP Suretrac limited slip differential, 10-inch ventilated front discs and AP Racing/Caterham four-pot alloy front callipers, quick-release Racetech steering wheel and wide-track front suspension. The wider track meant that only cycle wings could be fitted, and not flared wings. The gearbox was naturally Caterham's own close-ratio six-speed unit and the exhaust system a four-into-two-into-one system with a side-exit six-inch silencer.

Unique to the 'R' was a set of race-spec 13-inch Caterham Modular two-piece split-rim alloy wheels (6½J wide up front, 8½J to the rear) with semi-slick bespoke Avon ACB10 tyres (7 x 13-inch front, 8 x 13-inch rear). The nose cone and front cycle wings were in carbon fibre and the rest of the specification was ultra-lightweight in the best Superlight tradition (it was only 5kg heavier than the ordinary Superlight). So the R came with no windscreen (only a wind deflector), no spare wheel or carrier and no rear wing protectors (all these could be added if desired, at extra cost and weight).

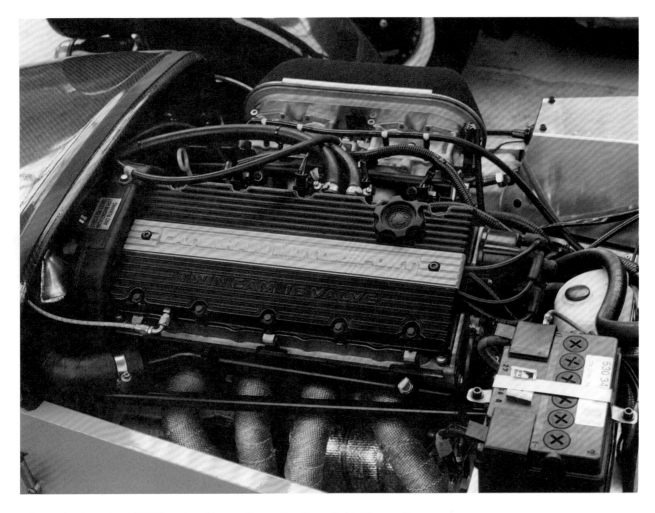

Launched at the 1997 London Motor Show, the Superlight R was then the most costly car in the range at £22,995 in kit form. To rave reviews (*Autocar* said it had 'quasi-racer handling, braking and steering responses'), the Superlight R quickly gained legendary status as a no-compromise super-fast projectile, capable of sub-4.0-second 0–60mph times.

But perhaps the R was too focused for anything but occasional road and track use. As John Barker in *Evo* magazine commented: 'I've always felt the original Superlight was a better driver's car . . . more tractable, more driveable with its narrower rear tyres and quite fast enough.' The ACB10 tyres were probably the main factor in such a conclusion, as they were much wider than other 7s; great for track work and on flat, dry roads, but very difficult on bumpy, cambered or wet roads. Caterham now fits the better-received tyres specified for the R500 in place of the ACB10.

Autocar broadly concurred with other press comments: 'The 7 is so frantic in its reactions to your input that . . . it is almost too harsh. Too mad.' The very close-ratio nature of the gearbox only contributed to the sense of full-on maniacal progress. Nevertheless, for the ultimate 7 buzz, the Superlight R was as extreme as it got. As a result of the uncompromising specification, demand for the R was restricted to a very select band of thrill-seekers and the Superlight R remained a very rare beast.

The 190bhp VHPD engine was a very special powerplant, with a nitro-carburised crankshaft, forged pistons, bigger cylinder head porting, larger valves, special camshafts and throttle body fuel injection. The Caterham Motorsport cam cover is gold.

Superlight R decals identified the highly specialised newcomer.

Classic spec 7 discovers Vauxhall power

Stockpiled supplies of new Ford crossflow engines eventually petered out in 1998. Caterham continued to offer the Classic without an engine for kit builders with engine mountings for a reconditioned Ford crossflow engine, but at the October 1997 London Motor Show Caterham announced that its new Classic would have an engine from an unexpected source – Vauxhall.

The new engine was the same capacity as the old Ford Kent engine (1.6 litres) and developed effectively the same power as the outgoing Sprint unit – 100bhp at 5,500rpm. It had notably more torque lower down the rev band, at 107lb ft at 3,600rpm (compared to the Sprint's 100lb ft at 4,500rpm).

In many ways this was an old-tech engine in the same spirit as the Ford units. It may have had an aluminium bell housing and sump, but the engine sported a mere eight valves, a single overhead camshaft, twin Weber 40DCOE carburettors and cast-iron construction. The head was polished and ported and the carbs were mounted on a bespoke Caterham alloy manifold. All of which made the new Classic VX an 'honest' 7 in the sense of it carrying on the tradition of no-nonsense performance.

One advance was that the Classic was now offered with at least five speeds. Instead of the old Classic's four speeds, the standard choice was

In 1998, the Classic model was reinvented when Caterham adopted the Vauxhall 1.6-litre engine in place of the Ford crossflow. It formed the basis of the Academy racing car.

Summary

New entry-level 7 engine comes from Vauxhall, and despite advances such as extra gear ratios and more equipment, it remains the no-frills grass roots choice.

Identifying features

Vauxhall 1600 engine, five or six-speed gearbox, live rear axle, first chassis number 30378.

The Vauxhall 1600 engine boasted the same power output as the old Ford Sprint engine (100bhp) but had more torque and a broader spread of torque low down.

the ubiquitous Ford Sierra V6 Type 9 five-speed unit (which was now out-of-production and therefore had to be sold as a reconditioned used item). You could choose Caterham's six-speed gearbox if you wished, but in this budget market it was a rare choice. The Classic specification was not quite as denuded as before, including full instrumentation, cloth seats, carpets, four-into-one competition exhaust and boot cover. Aero screens could be replaced with a windscreen at extra cost, and other options included weather gear, a heater and alloy wheels.

The new engine also dovetailed with the government's new Single Vehicle Approval (SVA) test regime for low volume cars. Owners could take their cars to SVA testing stations or Caterham would do it on their behalf. Most Classics were sold for amateur (kit) build, mainly because the Classic relied on a reconditioned live rear axle, although the rules still allowed for cars to be registered as new if they used only one second-hand item. The cost of the Classic was £10,995, and the same price applied to the Scholarship S series (later Academy) racer with the Vauxhall engine.

Specification	
Engine	Vauxhall 1600
Capacity	1,598cc
Bore x stroke	79.98 x 79.5mm
Induction	Twin Weber 40DCOE carburettors
Compression ratio	10.4:1
Max power	100bhp (75kW) at 5,500rpm
Max torque	107lb ft (145Nm) at 3,600rpm
Gearbox	Ford Sierra five-speed or Caterham six-speed
Brakes	9in front discs, 8in rear drums (10in ventilated front discs optional)
Steering	Rack-and-pinion
Weight	1,160lb (526kg)
Top speed	110mph (177kph)
0–60mph	6.7sec
50–70mph	N/A
Number produced	224 to date

1.8 K-series/Supersport/Roadsport

Caterham is first to the MGF engine

It was almost inevitable that Caterham would eventually offer the 1.8-litre K-series engine in the 7. When launching the 1.6-litre K-series car, it was thought that the longer-stroke 1.8-litre unit would not be as tuneable as the smaller engine, which was true; but more importantly, the 1.8-litre engine was simply not available for outside suppliers in 1996.

But there was clearly a market for a larger engine that offered greater torque and a less frenetic drive. Therefore, after extensive testing (Caterham was the first company outside Rover to be offered the 1.8-litre engine for testing), Caterham introduced it alongside the 1.6 unit in its range.

The 1,796cc engine came directly from the MGF and was the same unit fitted to the Lotus Elise so it already had plenty of acceptance. In its standard form it developed 124bhp at 5,700rpm but more significant was its extra torque: 122lb ft at 3,000rpm (versus 107lb ft for the 1.6). Overall it had a more relaxed power delivery and Caterham suggested that it 'would ideally suit those wishing to retain high performance with the ability for longer distance cruising.' Its spread of torque was also more suited to the five-speed gearbox.

As ever there was a Supersport conversion with bespoke engine management control and uprated camshafts, plus the welcome addition of a gear upchange light on the dashboard. The tuning yielded an extra 16bhp,

With the arrival of 1.8-litre K-series power, the 7 became rather grown-up. The torquier engine characteristics suited the Roadsport specification ideally (as pictured here).

Summary

Fitting the MGF's 1.8-litre engine gives the 7 more long-legged and torquey manners, as well as even better performance.

Identifying features

Caterham-branded Rover K-series 1800 engine, five or six-speed gearbox, de Dion rear axle, first chassis number 30380.

with the Supersport rated at 140bhp at 6,800rpm (and torque of 124lb ft at 5,250rpm), which was only 7bhp more than the 1600 Supersport engine.

So by 1998, Caterham had a closely stacked range of engines, with 1,600cc units of 101bhp, 115bhp and 133bhp, plus 1,800cc units of 124bhp, 140bhp, 150bhp and 190bhp. Quite a spread!

The 1.8 K-series installation was previewed at the 1997 London Motor Show for the 1998 model year. Prices started at £15,995 and it became the choice for owners wanting a more comfortable 'up-market' 7 with very good performance built in. An even more exciting 1.8-litre variant awaited in 1998 with the launch of the VVC-powered 7. All K-series powered 7s were rebranded as the Roadsport in 1999, to follow the rebranding of the race series in 1998.

Taken straight from the MGF, the 1.8-litre K-series engine developed 122bhp in standard form and 140bhp in Supersport tune.

Specification	
Engine	Rover K-series/Supersport
Capacity	1,796cc
Bore x stroke	80 x 89.3mm
Induction	Rover multi-point fuel injection
Compression ratio	10.5:1
Max power	122bhp (91kW) at 5,700rpm/140bhp (104kW) at 6,800rpm
Max torque	122lb ft (165Nm) at 3,000rpm/124lb ft (168Nm) at 5,250rpm
Gearbox	Ford five-speed or Caterham six-speed
Brakes	9in solid discs front and rear
Steering	Rack-and-pinion
Weight	1,200lb (544kg)
Top speed	118mph/120mph (190kph/193kph)
0-60mph	5.8/5.3sec
50-70mph	N/A
Number produced	Still in production

1.8 K-Series VVC/ VVC Roadsport

Variable valve power for a new 'luxury' 7

Caterham pulled quite a coup by launching a 7 powered by the MGF VVC engine at the March 1998 Geneva Motor Show, a full year before Lotus did the same with the Elise 111S. After more than a year of pleading to buy the engine to meet the need for an EU emissions-legal high-power unit, the 7 became the first car to be fitted with the VVC engine outside the Rover Group. The new Caterham-branded VVC engine extended the 7's horizons into uncharted territories of refinement and pulling power, unvisited since the days of the now-defunct Vauxhall HPC.

VVC stands for variable valve control, a system that uses hydraulic valve control to boost low-end torque without sacrificing top-end power. When accelerating the cam timing is extended to increase the volume of mixture entering the cylinders, providing a flat and consistent torque curve across the rev band. Power is a very healthy 150bhp at 7,000rpm – 7bhp higher than the MGF unit thanks to a new exhaust system – while the maximum torque of 128lb ft is delivered at 4,500rpm. Caterham fits its own sports exhaust system and lightweight clutch flywheel assembly, and the rev limiter comes in at 7,000rpm, lower than the Supersport engines. The engine itself weighs only 101kg and is an ideal choice from the emissions and noise point of view. Thus it has become the first choice for many export markets requiring emissions homologation.

When fitted with the Rover MGF 1.8 VVC engine, the 7 took on a more touring character, for the 150bhp new engine offered an impressive blend of power, torque and smoothness.

Summary

VVC engine takes the 7 into new territories of refinement and speed, making it the ideal everyday all-rounder and fully emissions legal across Europe.

Identifying features

Caterham-branded Rover K-series 1800 VVC engine, five or six-speed gearbox, de Dion rear axle, '16 valve' logo on badge, first chassis number 30422.

In Britain the VVC is sold with the five-speed gearbox, although the six-speed is also homologated (optional at £1,500 in the UK, standard in some export markets). Other popular options include wide-track front suspension, limited slip differential and uprated disc brakes. There is no Superlight-style rear anti-roll bar and softened steering responses. The base price was £18,495 at launch for an amateur-build version, or an extra £2,250 fully built, making it one of the most expensive 7s in the range.

This was effectively a 'luxury' 7 with the compliant suspension settings of the non-Superlight 7s, 15-inch Prisoner-style alloy wheels (16-inchers were optional), tonneau cover, heater, heated windscreen and padded leather seats. The suspension settings gave it great ride composure, especially over rough roads, at the expense of slightly less involving handling. Not strictly in the spirit of Colin Chapman's original 'light is best' philosophy, perhaps, but then there was and remains a very strong market for a 'Grand Touring' 7 that is perfectly useable on a regular basis.

As a replacement for the defunct Vauxhall-engined HPC, the VVC may have been less powerful and less torquey, but was still a very impressive drive. It offered a good blend of power and torque together, and was ideally suited to the driver who didn't want to rev an engine hard all the time. But it certainly rewarded the push-on driver; it may have lacked some of the low and mid-range pull of the HPC, but above 3,000rpm it was a different story. The 30–70mph sprint through the gears took a mere 4.9 seconds, almost the same as the HPC, and into Ferrari territory. One other bonus of the well-sorted Rover engine was fuel economy, with the potential to edge mpg into the low 30s.

Along with the rest of the K-Series range, the VVC model was regrouped under the Roadsport name in 1999. It has always remained a strong seller, with sales improving year-on-year.

Specification	
Engine	Rover K-series VVC
Capacity	1,796cc
Bore x stroke	80 x 89.3mm
Induction	Rover multi-point fuel injection
Compression ratio	10.5:1
Max power	150bhp (112kW) at 7,000rpm
Max torque	128lb ft (174Nm) at 4,000rpm
Gearbox	Ford Sierra five-speed or Caterham six-speed
Brakes	9in solid discs front and rear
Steering	Rack-and-pinion
Weight	1,200lb (544kg)
Top speed	126mph (203kph)
0-60mph	4.9sec
50-70mph	8.0sec
Number produced	Still in production

From 1996, the 7 came with new, separate seats and a new transmission tunnel with the handbrake sited centrally for the first time. Although Caterham-branded, the VVC engine (left) came virtually unaltered from Rover. It featured variable valve timing and a surprisingly rounded performance.

The new post-1996 dashboard featured Caterham-branded gauges.

Silverstone/40th Anniversary

Reviving the aluminium-bodied 7

The idea of an all-aluminium-bodied 7 harking back to the early Series 1 days of the Lotus 7 carries plenty of appeal. The Silverstone was just such a project, although it was not the first aluminium-bodied 7 offered by Caterham. Indeed, there had been two previous incarnations. The first (called the Jubilee) came in 1984 to celebrate 25 years of Caterham's association with the 7. It was seen at shows with its beautifully polished aluminium finish but was too expensive for anyone actually to buy one. Next came the so-called Lightweight in 1991, which was launched at the same time as the K-series 7. Once again the aluminium wings (cycle-type this time) and nose cone worked out rather expensive.

The difference with the Silverstone, launched at the 1998 Birmingham Motor Show, was that it was not simply a package of hand-beaten aluminium body panels. It was true that it, too, marked an anniversary – 25 years of 7 production at Caterham – but it went one stage further than previous all-metal bodied cars.

First it took the retro theme more seriously with extra cosmetic alterations. The dash layout echoed the Lotus Series 2, with a red lami-plate dashboard, while the rear lights were Series 2 type with separate indicators and Morris Minor-style brake/rear light clusters.

Secondly it adopted what was effectively an 'obsolete' engine - the 1700

The Silverstone was one of several attempts to market an all-aluminium bodied 7.

Summary

To celebrate 25 years of making the 7, Caterham's Silverstone is an all-aluminium throwback to the Series 2 Lotus 7 with 1700 Supersprint power.

Identifying features

Bored-out Supersprint engine with red cam cover, aluminium wings and nose cone, S2-style 'retro' dash and rear lights, UK chassis numbers 30645, 30651 and 30677 (last Japanese 40th Anniversary chassis 30602).

Ford Supersprint engine which was last of the crossflows to be fitted to a new Caterham. The Ford pushrod engine was chosen for its appeal to the traditionally minded 7 enthusiast, and for its long-standing link with the 7 (the crossflow was first fitted to a 7 some 20 years earlier). But the 135bhp engine was not in fact fitted to any customer cars. Instead, a bored-out Supersprint engine was used. With 1,760cc, a Kent 244 cam, increased ratio roller rockers and a red cam cover, it developed 146bhp rather than the 135bhp in 1,691cc guise and produced BDR-rivalling performance.

The aluminium-bodied Silverstone found just three UK buyers, each one fitted with the 146bhp engine. However, it formed the basis of a limited edition 40th Anniversary model for the Japanese market. Some 30 cars were supplied to what was basically Silverstone spec.

Although not productionised, the Silverstone led to this special limited edition aluminium 7 which was exported to Japan to say goodbye to the Supersprint crossflow engine. The Silverstone was not the first time an all-aluminium-bodied 7 had been offered. For example, below is an all-metal 7 at the Docklands launch of the K-Series Caterham in 1991.

Specification	
Engine	Modified Ford Supersprint
Capacity	1,760cc
Bore x stroke	86.7 x 77.62mm
Induction	Twin Weber 40DCOE
Compression ratio	9.5:1
Max power	146bhp (109kW) at 6,600rpm
Max torque	123lb ft (167Nm) at 5,400rpm
Gearbox	Ford Sierra five-speed or Caterham six-speed
Brakes	9in solid discs front and rear
Steering	Rack-and-pinion
Weight	1,300lb (590kg)
Top speed	118mph (190kph)
0-60mph	5.0sec
50-70mph in top:	N/A
Number produced	30

Classic VX Supersprint

The Vauxhall Supersprint engine was an expanded 1.8-litre version of the Vauxhall-powered Classic with 120–125bhp on tap.

Caterham tunes the Vauxhall engine

The Classic continued to be one of the most popular models at Caterham (now with the Vauxhall engine fitted). But with the demise of the old Ford Supersprint engine – for so many years the absolute mainstay of the 7 range – there was now a glaring gap in the range for a Supersprint replacement. Since the Sprint, there had always been a tuned version of the entry-level 7, so Caterham identified a need for a new 'grass roots' live axle 7 with a more powerful engine than the 101bhp Vauxhall-engined Classic.

At the October 1998 Birmingham Motor Show, Caterham addressed that gap. It launched a new Classic model with a larger Vauxhall engine. The 1.6-litre engine was bored out to 1.8 litres and fitted with larger pistons, reworked carburettors and different camshaft.

The new model was called the Classic Supersprint, borrowing its name from the classic eponymous Ford-engined model first seen in 1984 (in Caterham lexicography, Supersprint refers to carburettor-fed cars, while Supersport is for fuel-injected engines). The new engine had rejetted Weber carbs and a hotter camshaft.

The new Vauxhall Supersprint engine was not as powerful as the old Ford version, with 125bhp at 6,250rpm as opposed to 135bhp at 6,000rpm (the engine's power output was later revised down to 120bhp, although many Ford Supersprint engines certainly did not produce 135bhp as originally claimed). Interestingly, the Vauxhall Supersprint had precisely the same torque figure (122lb ft) as the Ford Supersprint.

Like the 1.6 Classic, the 1.8-litre version could be ordered with a live rear axle and five-speed gearbox (both remanufactured items) or with Caterham's own six-speed transmission. The 1.8 engine option cost an additional £1,255 in 2000, raising the price of a component-form Classic to £12,250.

Summary

Larger-engined and more powerful Classic Vauxhall 7 launched in 1998 is the spiritual successor to the great Ford Supersprint car.

Identifying features

Bored-out Vauxhall 1800 carb engine, five or six-speed gearbox, live rear axle, first chassis number 30691.

Specification

Engine	Caterham-modified Vauxhall 1800
Capacity	1,796cc
Bore x stroke	84.8 x 79.5mm
Induction	Twin Weber 40DCOE carburettors
Compression ratio	10.4:1
Max power	125bhp (93kW) at 6,250rpm (later 120bhp/89kW)
Max torque	122lb ft (165Nm) at 4,750rpm
Gearbox	Ford Sierra five-speed or Caterham six-speed
Brakes	9in front discs, 8in rear drums (10in ventilated front discs optional)
Steering	Rack-and-pinion
Weight	1,160lb (525kg)
Top speed	118mph (190kph)
0-60mph	5.8sec
50-70mph	N/A
Number produced	Approx 10 (up to November 2001)

ClubSport
Rare 7 specified for track days

The short-lived ClubSport was created with a specification to suit track day use, including a race roll-over bar, fire extinguisher and electrical cut-off switch.

Summary

Motorsports-orientated spec makes the ClubSport the ideal dual-purpose road/race weekend car.

Identifying features

Caterham-Rover K-series 1800 dry-sump engine, six-speed gearbox, race roll-over bar, fire extinguisher, electrical cut-off switch, chassis numbers within sequence 30628–30719.

Brand new at the October 1998 Birmingham Motor Show, where it debuted alongside the Silverstone and Classic Supersprint models, was the ClubSport. This was very much a range-topping newcomer with a strong emphasis on track use.

The idea came about because of the success of the Caterham Motorsport Club. This was a newly formed club which offered owners the opportunity of simply turning up in their 7 and participating in motorsports-orientated activities, including track days, handling courses and autotests. As well as providing demonstrations of how the 7 could perform, Caterham's track days were the perfect introduction to circuit driving, while the autotests provided a competitive element. Drivers would often approach Caterham asking what specification a track day car ought to have, so the company crystallised its ideas into one car, the ClubSport.

The specification was technically quite sophisticated, with a dry-sump oil lubrication system, uprated brakes (four-pot front callipers) and Caterham's six-speed transmission. The ClubSport came as standard with the 1.6-litre K-series Supersport unit, although two of the five cars built were fitted with 1.8-litre K-series engines. The exhaust system was rear-exit to keep noise down at circuits where decibel readings were taken.

Emphasising its alternative motorsports role, Caterham fitted the

Specification	
Engine	Caterham Rover Supersport
Capacity	1,588cc/1,796cc
Bore x stroke	80 x 79mm/80 x 89.3mm
Induction	Rover multi-point fuel injection
Compression ratio	10.5:1
Max power	133bhp (99kW) at 7,000rpm/140bhp (104kW) at 6,800rpm
Max torque	110lb ft (149Nm) at 5,000rpm/124lb ft (168Nm) at 5,250rpm
Gearbox	Caterham six-speed
Brakes	10in ventilated front discs, 9in solid rear discs
Steering	Rack-and-pinion
Weight	1,200lb (544kg)
Top speed	112mph/120mph (180kph/193kph)
0-60mph	6.0sec/5.3sec
50-70mph in 4th	4.7sec/N/A
Number produced	5

ClubSport with a race-style FIA roll-over bar, fire extinguisher and electrical cut-off switch, just like the official Caterham race series cars. The price also included free membership of the Caterham Motorsport Club and free track time for the driver to use at club events.

The idea for a track-day car was sound, but in the real world most drivers wanted to tailor their car to their own spec – for instance some wanted roll cages, some didn't. As Caterham also wanted to simplify what was becoming an increasingly complicated range, the ClubSport was quietly dropped after less than a year on the price lists and only five sales.

Caterham acknowledged the growing interest in cars used especially for track days, but found that owners really wanted to create and develop bespoke machines.

Superlight R500

500bhp per tonne for the fastest ever 7

Nothing short of a JPE had the Superlight R500's extraordinary pace. This was a devastating combination of feather weight, very high power and lightning sharp chassis.

Summary

Devastating successor to the JPE combines 230bhp power with ultra-light body to make the quickest roadgoing 7 ever built.

Identifying features

Caterham Motorsport branded K-series engine, much carbon fibre bodywork, aerofoil front wishbones, lightweight seats, ventilated front discs with four-pot callipers, six-speed gearbox, Stack display, special decals, first chassis number 30727.

By 1998, everyone at Caterham was sharply aware how much of a blast the JPE had been (it was now effectively defunct). The Superlight R was quick and focused but no true successor to the scorching JPE. The need for a genuine inheritor of the JPE's mantle was made more acute by the arrival of such high-profile newcomers as the Lotus 340R.

The Superlight R500 was an utterly convincing riposte, and probably the most driver-orientated car that Caterham has ever produced. With the first car built in August 1999, the R500 name reflected the car's stunning power-to-weight ratio of 500bhp per tonne.

That figure came courtesy of a very special engine. Based on the 1.8-litre Rover K-series, one of the main changes was to the induction. Inside a unique Caterham Motorsport inlet manifold, instead of a butterfly valve there were now roller barrel throttle bodies to improve airflow – a claimed world first on a production car – boosting power by at least 10bhp. Then there was a longer-lift asymmetrical camshaft, larger ports, forged steel con-rods and crankshaft, Cosworth forged-aluminium pistons and an 11.5:1 compression ratio. Add in a fully mapped MBE engine management system, compact injectors and a specially developed exhaust system and the power shot up to 230bhp at a screaming 8,600rpm – no less than 128bhp per litre. The maximum rev limit was set at no less than 9,000rpm.

Specification	
Engine	Caterham-developed Rover K-series
Capacity	1,796cc
Bore x stroke	80 x 89.3mm
Induction	Caterham Motorsport manifold with roller barrel actuation
Compression ratio	11.5:1
Max power	230bhp (172kW) at 8,600rpm
Max torque	155lb ft (210Nm) at 7,200rpm
Gearbox	Caterham six-speed
Brakes	10in lightweight ventilated discs front, 9in solid discs rear
Steering	Rack-and-pinion
Weight	1,014lb (460kg)
Top speed	146mph (235kph)
0-60mph	3.4sec
50-70mph	4.0sec
Number produced	94 to 2001

At the heart of the R500 was this highly developed K-series engine with an amazing 230bhp. Combined with an overall weight of 460kg, that gave the R500 its name; the power-to-weight ratio exceeded 500bhp per tonne.

Superlight-inspired weight-saving measures dropped the weight down to just 460kg (1,014lb), which was some 70kg (154lb) less than the JPE. Carbon fibre was used for the wings, nose cone, sill protectors, mirrors and dashboard, while even the wind deflector was now made of carbon fibre rather than Perspex. Each branded, minimally leather-trimmed carbon/Kevlar racing seat weighed half that of normal ones (later, the seat choice switched to bespoke carbon Kevlar racing style seats, which weighed a mere 2kg each – less than the runners they were mounted on!). The interior also featured a Stack digital instrument display with optional data logging.

The six-speed gearbox was mated to a lightweight magnesium bell housing, as was the weight-saving dry sump. The R500 also got a lightweight chassis (which was eventually adopted for other models in the range). The roll-over bar was broader but made of thinner gauge steel so it was no heavier.

Another change was the design of the front suspension wishbones, which were manufactured from aerofoil section tubing and were 30 per cent lighter than normal. They probably helped the aerodynamics too. Fabulous-looking, unique split-rim alloy wheels (magnesium centres, spun aluminium rims) were shod with bespoke Avon CR500 radial tyres (listed as 185 front, 215 rear but actually 175 front and 205 rear). These addressed criticisms of the ACB10 Superlight tyres, offering more all-round usability.

There were inevitable comparisons with the JPE, but the R500's performance was in fact even more crushing than the JPE, while the engine's power was far less peaky. It was difficult to describe the ferocity of the acceleration, but the figures were stark (0–30mph in 1.6 seconds, 0–60mph in 3.44 seconds, 0–100mph in 8.07 seconds). The 0–60 time was quick enough to confirm its place as the fastest-accelerating

For the first time the 7 got a Stack multi-function instrument display with optional data logging, as well as the usual Superlight carbon fibre treatment.

production car in the world in 2000. In its road test summary, *Autocar* said, 'The only production car ever built that would convincingly outgun the R500 is the McLaren F1 . . . the most exciting production car we've driven this year: a total blast.'

The engine also sounded fantastically intense, with an ability to rev beyond 9,000rpm. The fireworks did not really come into play until you were beyond 5,000rpm, but the narrow power band was never a problem because Caterham's six-speed gearbox worked so well with it. The gearing was very short (17.6mph per 1,000rpm) but that still equated to a theoretical top speed of 162mph – 146mph in reality! In-gear acceleration was also astonishing, with 30 – 70mph through the gears taking merely 2.6 seconds. It came as little surprise when an R500 smashed the lap record for production cars at the Nürburgring in 2000, at an amazing 7 minutes 54 seconds (on a damp track!). Despite the performance, the R500 was remarkably docile at engine speeds of 2,000rpm, something that you could never say of the JPE.

As for the driving experience, this was as close to a roadgoing race car as Caterham had yet come. Grip from the Avon tyres was almost beyond belief, although the power available could unleash slides at will. The Avon CR500 radial tyre was bespoke to the R500 and a far better all-rounder than the Superlight's ACB10; less prone to wet-weather loss of grip, and much less susceptible to tramlining on normal roads (the ACB10 was basically a road-legal Formula Ford crossply).

Unique 13-inch split-rim magnesium alloy wheels were specially developed for the R500, along with unique and highly acclaimed CR500 Avon tyres.

The R500's standard 10-inch ventilated front discs and AP Racing/Caterham four-pot callipers produced among the best brakes of any road car ever. Moreover, the R500 seemed to deliver a more rounded performance than the VHPD-engined Superlight R, with less of its hard-as-nails extremism. It was a manic experience, but it was far more accessible than the JPE that it effectively replaced, and a far better all-round car. Nevertheless, without a screen and with fairly uncomfortable seats, the R500 was still a short blast specialist only.

This was also a hellishly expensive 7, initially retailing at £30,000 in component form, or £2,250 more if you wanted it built, which was some £13,000 more than the Superlight 1.6 and £7,000 more than the Superlight R, but then this was the fastest Caterham yet made. It became instantly popular, selling as many in six months as it had taken the JPE six years to notch up.

Once again there was a special decal and plaque package for the R500, ensuring its exclusivity – although this was far more popular than the JPE had been.

An undiscovered secret for America

The 7 and Ford engines go hand-in-hand, of that there is no doubt. A huge variety of Ford powerplants has been used over the years, from the ancient sidevalve, Anglia 105E, Classic 109E, Kent crossflow and even the Escort CVH. But in recent times, Caterham has swayed to other engine suppliers, notably Vauxhall and Rover.

But there will always be many reasons why Ford power continues to be in demand – historic, practical, even romantic. Perhaps Caterham was edging back to the blue oval when, as a result of being forced to consider a powerplant for the American market, a Ford engine was chosen.

Ford pushrod engines had formed the mainstay of the American market, but from 1998 Caterham introduced the Ford Zetec 2.0-litre engine, well known in Europe in the Mondeo. But the engine was supplied to American specification, as fitted to the Ford Contour and Mercury Merkur, complete with variable valve timing. Great, you may think, but the exhaust camshaft VVT system was not fitted for extra power but as an emissions tool to avoid having to fit exhaust gas recirculation. The result was a clean powerplant that returned 135bhp at a fairly leisurely 5,500rpm. Not great, but better than the 128bhp standard output because of Caterham's exhaust system, and it was legal across 49 states for home assembly.

The installation was headed up by the US Caterham distributor John Nelson and signed off by Jez Coates, with the first production car assembled at Dartford then stripped and shipped to the USA. The chassis was a de Dion type, fitted with a five-speed Ford gearbox only. Because SCCA race regulations required flared wings, special widened clamshell wings had to be made to cover the wide front tyres (wide-track front suspension was not fitted, however, although the Watts linkage rear end was).

Described by Caterham's Jez Coates as 'one of the best kept secrets about the 7', Caterham hoped to exploit the US market far more with this car, and set up a *Road & Track* road test to highlight the model's existence.

There was also an SCCA-approved race version of the Zetec 7, which differed little from the road car except for a quick-ratio steering rack and a massively oversized and prodigiously heavy roll cage. This was very successful in categories that included heavily modified Mazda Miatas and the like. A Caterham Zetec was on pole for the year-end run-off race, for example.

In an effort to crack the difficult American market, Caterham developed a unique 7 fitted with a US-built Ford Contour 2.0 Zetec engine. It may have had 'only' 135bhp but it was fully legal across 49 states.

Specification	
Engine	US-spec Ford Zetec
Capacity	1,988cc
Bore x stroke	84.8 x 88.0mm
Induction	Ford multi-point fuel injection
Compression ratio	9.3:1
Max power	135bhp (101kW) at 5,500rpm
Max torque	130lb ft (176Nm) at 4,000rpm
Gearbox	Ford Sierra (Merkur) five-speed
Brakes	9in solid discs front and rear
Steering	Rack-and-pinion
Weight	1,170lb (530kg)
Top speed	N/A
0-60mph	N/A
50-70mph in top	N/A
Number produced	50 (up to 2001)

Summary

Ford Zetec power an ideal choice for the American market, and presaged Ford engines returning to UK and European cars.

Identifying features

US-spec Ford Zetec 2.0-litre engine, de Dion chassis, Ford five-speed gearbox, wide clamshell front wings, first chassis number 30620.

Caterham

7 Zetec (1998 to date)

V764 KKM

Autosport 50th Anniversary

Plush publisher's special edition

Something of an aberration perhaps in the unfolding 7 story, the Autosport 50th Anniversary 7 erred on the side of comfort with such items as an Alpine hi-fi as standard.

Summary

Autosport magazine wishes itself a very happy 50th birthday with a high-spec comfort-orientated official limited edition.

Identifying features

1.6 Supersport engine, red-and-gold paint scheme, decals and dash plaque, carbon fibre dash, Stack digital gauges, first chassis number 30775.

Specification

Engine	Rover K-series Supersport
Capacity	1,588cc
Bore x stroke	80 x 79mm
Induction	Rover multi-point fuel injection
Compression ratio	10.5:1
Max power	133bhp (99kW) at 7,000rpm
Max torque	110lb ft (149Nm) at 5,000rpm
Gearbox	Caterham six-speed
Brakes	10in ventilated front discs, 9in solid rear discs
Steering	Rack-and-pinion
Weight	1,212lb (550kg)
Top speed	120mph (193kph)
0-60mph	5.7sec
50-70mph in 4th	4.7sec
Number produced	9

As probably Britain's leading motorsports magazine, *Autosport* chose Caterham as the car on which to base a celebratory Anniversary model for its 50th year of publication in 2000. It secured the full support of Caterham Cars, who developed the new model to *Autosport* specifications. At its first showing at the 1999 *Autosport* dinner, the publishing manager of the magazine, Gordon Henderson, commented: 'The Caterham is a natural choice for *Autosport*, as it represents exactly the same values as our publication.'

The limited-availability new model – dubbed the Autosport 50th Anniversary Caterham – revelled in detail differences. The dashboard was covered in carbon fibre and featured a Stack digital instrument pod (with data logging optional). Other interior features included a Momo steering wheel, aluminium gear knob, leather seats, Caterham footwell mats and Caterham four-point harnesses. There was also a prominent red starter button in the centre of the dash.

One unusual piece of equipment was an Alpine CD stereo system, mounted ahead of the passenger. This was the only Caterham model fitted with this system, although for most 7 drivers the soundtrack of the engine obviated any need for a CD system.

A special paint scheme was employed: *Autosport* red with a gold band around the nose. 'Autosport 50' decals were positioned on each side of the bonnet. On the dashboard was a plaque attesting to the authenticity of the limited edition. Other extras included a year's subscription to the magazine, a year's membership of the Caterham Motorsports Club, a copy of *Autosport Circuit Guide*, Autosport 50th jacket and invitations to *Autosport* and Caterham events.

Described as 'the best compromise between road and race car', the basis for the car was the 1.6 Supersport with a six-speed gearbox, wide-track front suspension and HPC-type 16-inch five-spoke alloy wheels and Avon road tyres.

The new model was launched in January 2000 to widespread publicity in *Autosport* and its sister magazines within the Haymarket Publishing stable. The price tag for the limited-production Autosport 50th Anniversary Caterham was fairly high at £21,995 on the road, the limited edition being available during the year 2000 and into 2001.

Blackbird

Superbike and Super 7 come together

Britain's specialist car industry discovered superbike engines in the late 1990s. What could be more suited to a lightweight sports car than a lightweight engine that could rev into five figures – and with a sequential six-speed gearbox to suit?

The first 7 with a Blackbird engine was built by Paul Harvey and Doug Newman (of the Four Wheeled Motorcycle Company). Caterham looked at the project and took the idea on board and created its first bike-engined prototype in February 1999. It chose the Honda Blackbird CBR1100XX after vetting a number of alternative superbike engines. Acknowledged as one of the great 'bike engines of all time, the Blackbird was a 1.1-litre in-line four-cylinder 16V DOHC powerplant that delivered 170bhp at a screaming 10,750 revs – an astonishing 150bhp per litre. And the red line came up at 11,750rpm!

Unlike the first Blackbirds built, the official Caterham-built model switched carburettors for later-spec fuel injection. The exhaust was a large bore four-into-two-into-one system in stainless steel with a side-exit silencer.

Honda's six-speed sequential gearbox was an added bonus, with ultra-close ratios but very low-geared top to take maximum advantage of the rev band. Operated by a push-pull lever in the normal position, it worked

Caterham invested much time and effort to productionise its first motorbike-engined 7, the Blackbird. In character it recreated much of what the R500 was about. Although not as quick around a track, it was a lot cheaper.

Summary

Honda Blackbird superbike power transforms the 7 into a screaming projectile that is ideally suited to track day work.

Identifying features

Honda Blackbird engine and sequential six-speed gearbox, Superlight R500 seats and interior, chassis numbers within sequence 30869–10223.

Specification	
Engine	Honda Blackbird
Capacity	1,137cc
Bore x stroke	79 x 58mm
Induction	Honda fuel injection with throttle bodies and Ram Air
Compression ratio	11.0:1
Max power	170bhp (127kW) at 10,750rpm
Max torque	92lb ft (125Nm) at 8,250rpm
Gearbox	Honda six-speed sequential
Brakes	9in solid discs front and rear
Steering	Rack-and-pinion
Weight	970lb (440kg)
Top speed	132mph (212kph)
0-60mph	3.9sec
50-70mph in top	N/A
Number produced	5 (to date)

This is the prototype Blackbird car built by Paul Harvey and Doug Newman. Caterham was sufficiently impressed with its performance that it productionised the design.

The Honda CBR1100 Blackbird engine was a mighty powerplant, boasting 170bhp from just 1,137cc. A sequential six-speed gearbox was a welcome corollary of using the engine.

extremely well, the only caveat being rather long clutch travel and a very sharp action, despite the bespoke AP hydraulics. Reverse was easily selected via an electro-pneumatic mechanism; having a reverse gear is a legal requirement in the UK but it remains surprising how many other bike-engined cars neglect this obvious fact.

This extraordinary 7 variant was extensively trial-tested, including many miles of track-testing at the Estoril circuit in Portugal in the hands of BAR Formula 1 driver, Ricardo Zonta. It was said that 18,000 miles of race testing had proven the Blackbird installation – as the new 7 had been extensively campaigned (for example, scoring a class victory in the June 2000 Nürburgring 24-hour endurance race). It would also become eligible for a 750 Motor Club race series for bike-engined cars.

In essence the Blackbird shared much of its specification with the Superlight R500. You had the Stack dash information system, sequential shift lights, R500 composite seats (adjustable on the driver's side), there was a road-specification roll-over bar, while the dash and interior trim were made of carbon fibre. However, you did not get Superlight-type carbon fibre wings or nose cone (these were optional). There was a Superlight wind deflector in lieu of a windscreen, and no spare wheel, carrier or rear wing protectors. You could add these as options, as well as a windscreen, weather equipment and heater if you wished, but that all added weight as well as cost.

Other Superlight features included wide-track adjustable front suspension and adjustable anti-roll bars, Avon CR500 175/55

Here, Jordan Formula 1 star Jarno Trulli pilots the special-liveried Blackbird around Donington Park race circuit.

R13 tyres. To match the lower engine weight, the front springs were softer than K-series engined cars. There was a Honda engine immobiliser too.

The Blackbird received the best possible launch in the summer of 2000. In July, during a Caterham-organised corporate event for F1 team BAR, Ricardo Zonta conducted a press launch at Estoril, while in September, two cars in identical Jordan Formula 1 team liveries, were driven in front of crowds at the Donington race circuit 10th birthday party of the Jordan F1 Team. The pilots? None other than F1 drivers Jarno Trulli and Thomas Enger. At both events, the car was liveried up in the appropriate sponsorship colours (BAR Lucky Strike and Jordan Benson & Hedges).

The Blackbird was principally aimed at the burgeoning track day market, the sales brochure professing: 'This car is most at home lapping the circuits of Europe'. It added: 'but this by no means makes the car exclusive for the circuit – this fully road-legal car is as happy on the country B roads as it is breaking lap records.'

Autocar magazine agreed when it pitched the Blackbird into its 0–100mph–0 challenge. The Caterham accelerated up to the ton and back to rest in just 16.69 seconds, and the verdict on the bike-powered 7 was 'awesome'. Getting the car off the line cleanly was a challenge, as the power delivery was so ferocious, but once in the upper rev bands, in-gear acceleration was phenomenal. The gearbox in particular was a delight, with sharp-shifting changes that had you believing you were a BTCC driver. Most importantly, the lightness of the engine/box endowed the 7 with a cornering delicacy that was peerless, even among 7 variants.

It is frankly not the most practical choice for a number of reasons, mainly the highly tuned nature of the engine. It's great to drive flat-out, but in traffic the go-ahead engine character and very sharp clutch action with drivetrain backlash militates against it. It is also a very noisy machine, with a very loud exhaust and plenty of transmission whine.

One strange record held by the Blackbird was the fastest car in reverse; because the six-speed transmission worked in reverse too, sixth gear yielded a back-to-front maximum speed of 85mph on BBC's TV programme, *Record Breakers* (later bettered by the Fireblade at 102mph).

The cost of putting the Blackbird into production was relatively high, as was sourcing the Honda engine. As a result, the standard car cost £25,750 fully built – a lot less than the R500 but still rather expensive. Only five factory-built Blackbird cars had been supplied in the first year, with a further seven chassis set up for Blackbird engines.

Another picture of the Blackbirds that were painted in Jordan's yellow F1 colours at the event which celebrated 10 years of the Jordan team.

SV

Wider, longer 7 changes Chapman's shape for the first time

'Never change the shape of the 7' was the unwritten rule of Chapman's original. But that's just what Caterham did with the SV, a longer and wider 7 for larger customers.

Summary

A 7 to fit all sizes, the SV has greater cockpit length and width, plus more foot room, for a negligible weight disadvantage – a 7 for the new millennium?

Identifying features

Widened and lengthened chassis, bigger footbox, wide-track front suspension, Roadsport spec, taller windscreen, larger soft-top, first chassis number 50000.

One thing that never changed on the 7 for over 40 years was its basic shape and external dimensions – an absolutely critical factor in the model's continued success. But in a bold move, Caterham struck out in a new direction at the October 2000 Birmingham Motor Show, when the SV was launched – which Caterham described as 'the first-ever all-new Caterham 7'.

The reason for the SV was that the 7 was basically designed around Colin Chapman's 5ft 7in frame. During the years that Caterham had been producing the 7, the pedals had been moved forward, the seats moved back and the tunnel made narrower, so there was nothing else to be done to increase cockpit space. With a population that was growing ever taller and broader, many potential customers still had to skip the 7 because they simply didn't fit.

It became obvious that a bigger car was needed, so the SV was given an extra 3in (80mm) of cockpit length and 4.3in (110mm) of cockpit width. This all meant six-footers were an easy fit, and even the broad-hipped could now sqeeze in; there were additionally wider seats for full support (an MGF was used as the benchmark for seat width).

Equally importantly the changes yielded up a larger footbox, with an extra

128

Specification	
Engine	Rover K-Series 1.6 (any current 7 engine can be fitted)
Capacity	1,588cc
Bore x stroke	80 x 79mm
Induction	Rover multi-point fuel injection
Compression ratio	10.5:1
Max power	115bhp (86kW) at 6,000rpm
Max torque	107lb ft (145Nm) at 3,000rpm
Gearbox	Ford five-speed or Caterham six-speed
Brakes	9in solid discs front and rear (10in ventilated front discs optional)
Steering	Rack-and-pinion
Weight	1,268lb (575kg)
Top speed	122mph (196kph)(1.8)
0-60mph	5.3sec (1.8)
50-70mph in top	N/A
Number produced	40 (up to November 2001)

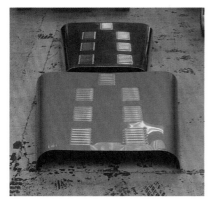

A far wider bonnet was fitted to the SV (in the foreground).

This is what the SV is all about: extra footroom, extra legroom and additional width to the seats. It enabled people to drive the 7 who could never have fitted it before.

2.2in (55mm) of width and 1in (25mm) of height. Generously shod shoe wearers could now have the confidence to flash between the pedals without worrying about catching more than one at the same time!

This was Caterham's biggest engineering project since the 21. To get to the SV (which stands for Special Vehicle) Caterham tried making all dimensions bigger, but it looked wrong. Computer manipulation eventually succeeded in tweaking the dimensions so that the car was bigger without looking ill-proportioned; great care was taken to preserve the original 7's looks. Most of the increase was in the width, and a wider radiator grille, wider and taller windscreen and modified weather gear were perhaps the most obvious external giveaways.

Overall, the new car had a track of 1,446mm (110mm more than other 7s) and a wheelbase of 2,305mm (80mm more, all added in the tube that you stepped over to get in). Wide-track 'Supersports' front suspension and Watts linkage rear were standard on the SV, there was a wider steering rack and a larger (9.1 gallon) fuel tank, but the extra length did not pose a problem for the propshaft, because the old Ford prop was long enough. Despite the extra size, there was only a 25kg weight penalty over a standard model.

It was intended that the SV chassis should be specified for all current Caterham models, but in the event it was only offered in Roadsport guise at prices from £16,250. Fully built cars cost £1,250 more than kit-built ones. The standard engine was the 1.6 K-series, but any engine could, in theory, be fitted, and a couple of early cars had 190bhp VHPD power.

Auto Express magazine's verdict was: 'the best just got bigger'. *Evo* magazine commented: 'the SV has lost nothing in, quite literally, broadening its appeal.' The SV was successfully subjected to full durability testing at Millbrook proving ground to a more rigorous standard than major manufacturers. The SV drove very much like any other 7, looked very much like any other 7 and had a genuine appeal for more people. It was no surprise that the SV was an immediate success. The first deliveries took place in 2001, with over 50 orders taken up until November 2001 with 40 units supplied. In particular, the SV looked a strong prospect for the American market, where the first LHD SV was shipped.

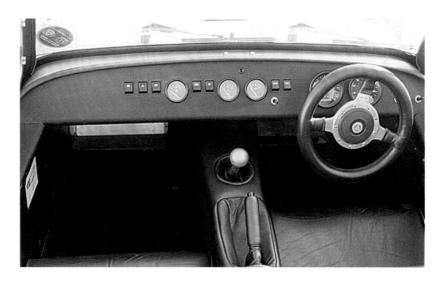

129

Fireblade

Better value superbike-engined option

The 919cc RRW 125–128bhp quad-carburettor engine helped to keep the car's weight below 400kg, making the Fireblade the lightest 7 ever produced.

Very much following in the footsteps of the Blackbird-powered 7, 2001 saw the introduction of an another superbike-powered Caterham. While the Blackbird occupied a rarefied position at the top of the track-day pecking order, the new Fireblade was to be a cheaper route into track day fireworks, costing from £17,000 fully built, or £15,000 in component form.

As its name suggests, the Fireblade used the engine, ancillaries and gearbox from another of Honda's superbikes, the CBR900 FireBlade. This impressive high-performance engine, first seen in 1992, evolved through several generations. To keep costs down, used bike engines were ideal (the 919cc RRW 125–128bhp quad-carburettor unit, although the expanded fuel injected version launched in 2000 was possible for future use).

The chassis was based on the live axle Seven to keep costs down. In fact, the live axle was an ideal choice; its one weakness was an intolerance of high torque, which of course bike engines do not have.

The budget spec meant that the Firebird lacked many of the Superlight features that distinguished the Blackbird, such as the carbon fibre interior trim set. Options included carbon wings and nose cone, uprated front brakes, windscreen, weather equipment, FIA roll-bar and limited slip differential.

Unlike the Blackbird, this was not to be an official Caterham product, but

Summary
Less expensive road/track day alternative to the Blackbird using Honda superbike power – an ultra-light, highly focused machine.

Identifying features
Honda FireBlade engine and sequential six-speed gearbox, live axle chassis, first chassis number 10267.

Specification	
Engine	Honda CBR900 RRW FireBlade
Capacity	919cc/929cc
Bore x stroke	71 x 58mm/74 x 54mm
Induction	Four Keihin 38 carburettors/fuel injection
Compression ratio	11.1:1/11.3:1
Max power	125-128bhp (94-95kW) at 10,500rpm/150bhp (112kW) at 11,500rpm
Max torque	67-68lb ft (91-92Nm) at 8,500rpm/76lb ft (103Nm) at 11,000rpm
Gearbox	Honda six-speed sequential
Brakes	9in solid discs front and rear
Steering	Rack-and-pinion
Weight	880lb (400kg)
Top speed	130mph
0-60mph	3.8sec
50-70mph in top	N/A
Number produced	10 (up to November 2001)

By using a live axle chassis and a less expensive second-hand 125bhp Honda FireBlade superbike engine, much of the Blackbird experience was recreated at a much lower price.

a factory-endorsed project. It was conceived and engineered by Paul Harvey, and sales and servicing of the Fireblade was exclusively by James Whiting Sevens, a long-established specialist in 7s. Caterham gave the green light for the project in April 2001, and extensive testing took place at the Nürburgring. Caterham supplied bespoke Fireblade chassis to James Whiting.

Perhaps the most remarkable thing about the 7 Fireblade was its weight. Thanks to the very light motorcycle components used, overall weight ducked below 400kg, a remarkable figure that ranked it as the lightest 7 ever made – even including the skimpy Lotus 7 Series 1. This gave it a power-to-weight ratio of 325bhp per ton.

As supplied, the Fireblade was specified for track day use, although it was still road legal. Customers wishing to broaden its appeal could fit options such as a full screen, weather equipment and heater, which naturally added weight. As for value, the starting price was deliberately kept low by basing the car on a live axle chassis and using second-hand motorcycle parts, which were relatively easy to come by, and a remanufactured rear axle. Deliveries began in Autumn 2001.

The Fireblade received huge press adulation, including being voted 'Track Car of the Year' by *Evo* magazine; even though the R500 might have been quicker, in terms of handling the Fireblade got the nod.

Beaulieu
Run-out Classic special edition

With an enhanced Classic specification, the Beaulieu was effectively a great value run-out edition of the Vauxhall-powered Classic.

Summary

Run-out Classic limited edition offers great value and the last chance to buy a Vauxhall-powered 7, plus a dash of Beaulieu kudos.

Identifying features

Vauxhall 1600 engine, live rear axle, Beaulieu dash plaque, yellow and green colour scheme, first chassis number 22059.

Specification

Engine	Vauxhall 1600
Capacity	1,598cc
Bore x stroke	79.98 x 79.5mm
Induction	Twin Weber 40DCOE carburettors
Compression ratio	10.4:1
Max power	100bhp (75kW) at 5,500rpm
Max torque	107lb ft (145Nm) at 3,600rpm
Gearbox	Ford Sierra five-speed or Caterham six-speed
Brakes	9in front discs, 8in rear drums (10in ventilated front discs optional)
Steering	Rack-and-pinion
Weight	1,160lb (526kg)
Top speed	110mph (177kph)
0-60mph	6.7sec
50-70mph	N/A
Number produced	20 (up to November 2001)

In 2001, Caterham Cars teamed up with the National Motor Museum at Beaulieu to create a limited edition 7 called the Caterham Beaulieu. Based on the Vauxhall-engined Classic model, it was both a reinvention of an entry-level 7 that customers might have been neglecting, and a hark back to the days of the Lotus 7 in terms of appearance and value.

The standard Beaulieu colour scheme was British Racing Green cycle wings and nose cone with a natural aluminium body finish and a yellow band on the nose cone. Each car came with its own individual dash plaque, signed by Lord Montagu of Beaulieu and was also supplied with a 'Limited Edition Caterham Beaulieu Pack'. This comprised a signed copy of Lord Montagu's autobiography, a certificate of authenticity, privilege passes to the museum and Bucklers Hard, membership of the Friends of the National Motor Museum, Beaulieu catalogues and a 'special gift' from Lord Montagu.

This was not the first time that Caterham and Lord Montagu had worked together. A 7 was often the first prize in a raffle to raise money at Beaulieu, and to commemorate the arrival of the new model, the National Motor Museum launched a competition with car chassis number one as first prize. It was put on display at the museum until October 2001, with the winner's ticket drawn at the International Classic Car Show in Birmingham.

In mechanical terms, the specification was very much Vauxhall Classic, with its twin carburettor-fed 1.6-litre eight-valve engine with polished and ported head and alloy manifold, live axle chassis, five-speed gearbox (six-speed optional) and drum rear brakes.

Unlike the Classic, the Beaulieu came with a full windscreen and weather gear, plus a Shurlock immobiliser. Caterham said that the Beaulieu had 'reinvented the entry-level Caterham, with prices starting from only £11,495. Seven motoring has never been such fantastic value.' That was certainly true, as the extras fitted greatly exceeded the £500 surcharge over a standard Classic.

The Beaulieu can be seen as the run-out edition of the Vauxhall-powered Classic, as the supply of engines was running out. Caterham envisaged that no more than around 50 Beaulieu cars would be built.

The press seemed to agree that this spec worked. *Auto Express* magazine lined up the 7 Beaulieu alongside the Lotus Exige, Honda S2000 and BMW M Coupé in an attempt to find the 'Most Fun Car'. The Caterham Beaulieu came first, ahead of the much more expensive Lotus, BMW and Honda.

7 kits

The usual way to buy a new Caterham is either in complete knock-down form or as a basic kit. The CKD option uses all-new parts, while the kit will usually be completed using some second-hand components to keep build costs down. Quality is always impeccable with a Caterham.

Summary

Thousands of Caterhams have been kit-built since 1984 – all to the same high quality manufacturing standards, but less certain is the provenance of the mechanical side and the competence of the individual build-up.

In an era of the glassfibre-bodied 'special' sold as a simple body tub, the Lotus 7 was a true beacon. Born as one of Britain's first true complete kit cars, it was always sold in complete component form with every item needed to finish a car supplied new. When Caterham took over the 7, it sold the car just as Lotus had sold it, in a comprehensive package of parts consisting of all-new components. Using new parts and supplying absolutely everything needed to build the car made the Caterham seem expensive alongside cheaper kit-built rivals in the early 1980s, when there was an explosion of interest in kit cars in Britain. This was the main reason why, in 1984, Caterham turned the clock back and began offering true kits – basic packages for home construction – in addition to component-form cars.

Caterham launched a basic body/chassis kit for just £1,850 plus VAT in 1984. This was just the beginning, as you then needed to add various trim and mechanical packages from Caterham, bringing the price up to £3,250, or £1,250 more with literally everything supplied except the engine, gearbox, rear axle, wheels and tyres. This price was substantially less than component-form 7 and yet kits were a lot more complete than most rivals; few could boast ready-fitted brakes, fuel tank, instruments, switches, wiring, windscreen and wipers. While Caterham quoted a 20-hour build time for the component-built car and 70 hours for the less fully-built

Caterham offers to inspect your car once it has been built. If you're buying a used kit-built car, always ask whether this check has been done.

Building a 7 from a kit is not necessarily a difficult task, merely time-consuming. No special tools are required other than an engine hoist and a 200lb ft torque wrench if you are building a de Dion car.

A basic kit takes around 150 hours to build, compared with 70 hours in CKD form and 20 hours in component form. One of the beauties of a 7 is that it is so easy to work on and restore.

complete knock-down (CKD) car, the pure kit build time was more like 150 hours.

Three chassis types were initially offered: short cockpit/Ford live axle; long cockpit/Ital axle, and long cockpit de Dion. (The short cockpit was eventually dropped in 1992.) Kits were immediately popular and within three years the majority of UK sales were by this means. The front-end cost saving was the main impetus behind this success, made all the more attractive by the avoidance of Car Tax in Britain because second-hand parts were used. Almost all kit-built cars were required to wear a 'Q' prefix registration plate, indicating the use of parts that were not new.

Of course, cars supplied in kit or CKD form do not have the same kudos as factory-built cars. But despite the fact that the factory did not advertise or publicise the availability of kits very heavily, kits and CKD units were extremely popular with domestic buyers, with numbers growing from 82 in 1985 up to 571 in 1990, the most prolific year for Caterham sales. This represented a greater than 2:1 ratio in overall production in favour of kits over factory cars. This also means that a majority of used 7s – from the late 1980s onwards – will be kit-built.

The very fact that used parts were fitted makes the purchase of a second-hand kit-built Caterham more risky. You often have no idea of the history of some major mechanical items prior to installation. It's best to assume that they will need recommissioning. Also you are more at the whim of the original builder's skills, so take more care over basic checks. Caterham did offer the facility of checking the build standards of kit cars at the factory, but not everyone took this up. So you should always ask for documentary evidence that the factory check was completed.

Another factor is that individual kit builders may deviate from standard specifications. While all the major safety items such as chassis, suspension, fuel tank and so on will be genuine Caterham parts, there is leeway for alternative specifications in some areas.

In particular, there is a likelihood that owners have used non-recommended engine/transmission combinations. It's quite common to see Caterhams with all sorts of engines, from Toyota to Alfa Romeo, Ford Zetec to Mazda rotary. One brave soul has even fitted a twin-turbo Rover V8! These should be treated with caution because, as previously stated, Caterham does not recommend non-standard engine installations, the engine mountings may be incorrect and the rest of the chassis set-up may be inappropriate for the engine weight and power.

While it may be tempting to look at a car with a very powerful but non-standard engine, specially cut gear ratios, 'racing' steering rack and myriad other 'desirable' features, the chances are that the balance of the 7 will have been upset in some way by such an approach, unless the builder is a very talented engineer with the sort of resources Caterham has at its disposal. Such cars need to be priced accordingly.

In conclusion, *caveat emptor* applies even more strictly to used kit-built Caterhams. Make thorough checks and you should avoid coming unstuck – indeed, you might even net yourself a great bargain.

Rebodied 7 gets an injection of practicality

Over its 40-year plus tenure of the 7, the one lesson that Caterham has learnt is never to alter the shape of Chapman's inspired sports car. But the 7 increased in popularity to such an extent that Caterham began to consider another model to go alongside it. It considered reviving the original Lotus Elan and even taking over other existing small car projects.

But Caterham would eventually settle on a new model of its own. With the 7 having passed low-volume type approval, plus noise and emissions tests, Caterham could finally contemplate tackling this major project in the mid-1990s.

Graham Nearn had always wanted to produce an all-enveloping car body like the Lotus 11. Project C21 was instigated to this effect, its name reflecting the fact that it would appear in Caterham's 21st year as a car manufacturer. For reasons of packaging and simplicity, it was decided to base the 21 on the 7 chassis, keeping the same wheelbase and rear track, and therefore the existing axle and drive shaft configuration. The rear suspension, engine and gearbox transferred straight over. The front track was widened by three inches to match the rear, benefiting handling and footbox space. The wide-track suspension was not the same as the wide-

The 21 marked a major new departure for Caterham Cars. Iain Roberton's delicately crafted shape was widely admired.

Summary

Attractive enveloping bodywork over the 7 chassis creates an all-new model that is more practical to live with, but has not caught on with buyers.

Identifying features

Wide-front 7 chassis, Iain Robertson designed bodywork in glassfibre or aluminium, curved windscreen, unique interior, hinged opening panels.

The new 21 badge echoed the design of the 7's. After all, under the skin the chassis was essentially that of a 7.

track 7, for the 21 simply widened the chassis at the front end while retaining the wishbones; the Superlight did the opposite by keeping the chassis the same but widening the wishbones. A new anti-roll bar was also designed for the 21, and spring and damper rates adjusted to suit what would be a heavier car.

The front chassis was altered by making the longitudinals run straight back. But to maintain stiffness, the sills remained high, a factor which would later be criticised in a car which purported to be semi-practical.

The 21 threw out the dogma that the exterior shape should not be touched but anything underneath could be changed to improve dynamics. The 21 kept the chassis basically unaltered but completely changed its bodywork!

Caterham has always erred on the side of driving pleasure rather than practicality, so the 21 got small doors, high sills and non-winding windows. Iain Robertson was called on to design the shape as early as 1993. Certain inspiration came from the Lotus 11, with much of the bodywork appearing to stretch membrane-like over the chassis. Virtually everyone agreed that the styling was a great success.

Proprietary lights were used to keep budgets reasonable, including Ford Mondeo rear lights and Suzuki Cappuccino indicators. Internal door handles came from the Rover 100 and mirrors from the Rover 200. A special windscreen was tooled up for. The 21's interior was every bit as exciting as the exterior. Separate 'nacelles' enveloped each passenger, while the 7's instruments were grouped vertically in a narrow centre console.

The prototype was built spectacularly out of polished aluminium, and made a huge impression at its debut, the October 1994 Birmingham Motor Show.

The first car was fitted with nothing less than a JPE engine and six-speed

Dynamically the 21 lost none of the sharpness of its 7 brother, and it was universally praised by road testers. However, its higher price forced comparisons with its closest contemporary, the Lotus Elise.

Although it was no wider between the sills, elbow room was much improved over the 7. The design and approach of the cockpit was an entirely fresh avenue.

Specification	21
Engine	Rover K-series 1.6 Supersport (other engines available)
Capacity	1,588cc
Bore x stroke	80 x 79mm
Induction	Rover multi-point fuel injection
Compression ratio	10.5:1
Max power	133bhp (99kW) at 7,000rpm
Max torque	110lb ft (149Nm) at 5,000rpm
Gearbox	Ford Sierra V6 five-speed or Caterham six-speed
Brakes	10in ventilated front discs, 9in solid rear discs
Steering	Rack-and-pinion
Weight	1,466lb (665kg)
Top speed	127mph (204kph)
0-60mph	6.7sec
50-70mph in top	7.9sec
Number produced	49

Dimensions (7 in brackets)	
Length	153.8in/3,800mm (133in/3,380mm)
Width	62.2in/1,580mm (62in/1,570mm)
Wheelbase	88.5in/2,225mm (88.5in/2,225mm)
Front track	53.1in/1,350mm (53.1in/1,350mm 7 wide-track)
Rear track	53.1in/1,350mm (53.1in/1,350mm)

Specification	21 GTO
Engine	Rover K-series Superlight R500
Capacity	1,796cc
Bore x stroke	80 x 89.3mm
Induction	Caterham Motorsport manifold with roller barrel actuation
Compression ratio	11.5:1
Max power	230bhp (172kW) at 8,600rpm
Max torque	155lb ft (210Nm) at 7,200rpm
Gearbox	Caterham six-speed
Brakes	10in lightweight ventilated discs front, 9in solid discs rear
Steering	Rack-and-pinion
Weight	1,543lb (700kg)
Top speed	153mph (246kph)
0-60mph	3.8sec
50-70mph in top	N/A
Number produced	1

gearbox. In this form, it was tested by some car magazines and TV programmes. *Autocar* said: 'The basic feel of the car is right . . . unmistakably Caterham. It is, if you like, a Seven without the strings . . . It is pulverisingly quick . . . There is much less buffeting, much better visibility and a greater sense of security.'

Aluminium was an expensive option to the standard body choice of composite material (moulded by Rawlsons in Kent). The original aluminium show car was sold to the Japanese Caterham distributor, and only one other aluminium car was built. Other engineering challenges for the 21 included curved glass, minimising panel gaps, creating hinges, locks, opening panels, doors and windscreen bonding. Practicality was certainly enhanced by the hinging boot (at 250 litres, it was able to contain the obligatory two sets of golf clubs) and Caterham even made a bespoke luggage set for the 21. And 7 owners never had an adjustable steering column or remote bonnet release!

The launch price was £18,750 in component form (called Clubman). The Vauxhall engine would not be fitted to any production cars; instead, the Rover K-series became the standard powerplant in the form of the 115bhp 1.6-litre unit. The 133bhp Supersport engine package was priced at an additional £999, while other options included the six-speed gearbox, 1.8 VHPD 190bhp engine, special paintwork and lightweight aluminium bodywork.

Weight was certainly impressive, with an all-up kerb weight of 1,466lb (665kg) – even lighter than the Lotus Elise (723kg). Its much improved aerodynamics (Cd 0.37 compared with 0.66 in a 7) helped out at higher speeds and the Supersport-powered 21 was capable of 127mph in sixth gear. Road tests revealed sprightly acceleration in this form, but not quite in the 7 league: 0–60mph in 6.7 seconds and 30–70mph through the gears at 6.3 seconds. The Supersport engine lacked the torque to do genuine battle with rivals such as the 1.8-litre Lotus Elise.

But in other respects the 21 was a delight to pilot: wrist-flick gearchanges, razor-sharp throttle response, intimate driving environment and superb brakes to name a few. In terms of handling, the heavier 21

Caterham 21 (1995 to date)

The hinged opening panels
marked a new challenge for
Caterham. Practicality was a
strong selling point for the
21; for example, golf clubs
could be fitted in the boot.

suffered a little by comparison with the 7. In particular the steering was
heavier and lacked a little feel, partly because of the extra weight but also
the wider, 205 section tyres. Grip was excellent but understeer was more
prevalent than the 7, with less propensity for controllable drifting at low
speeds. However, ride quality was notably better than a 7 and in ultimate
terms the enjoyment factor was still huge. This was in part due to the ultra-
stiff chassis, some 150 per cent stronger than the 7's.

Crucially, however, the 21 was inevitably compared with the Lotus Elise,
another lightweight two-seater that sold for around the same price. With a
development budget some 20 times higher than the 21's, it was almost
inevitable that the Lotus got the nod in most back-to-back tests, allied to
which everyone agreed that in the Elise Lotus had done its best work for a
whole generation. The 21 was even harder to get into than an Elise and its
cockpit width was determined by the same high sills that kept the 7 so
tight. The weather gear was fiddly, there was no space for a stereo and the
side windows could only be removed by undoing some screws. It was a
noisy beast, too, reflecting its purist origins and philosophy.

The maximum production capacity for the 21 was around 250 units a year
but no-one seriously anticipated this production volume. In fact, the 21
never became a big seller, the main reason being that it had so much
competition from new arrivals such as the Lotus Elise, Renault Sport Spider,
MGF, BMW Z3 and Honda S2000.

During its brief years in production, the 21 did not really evolve, and
although the first 18 months saw a programme of production
rationalisation, the product itself did not change. Only 49 cars were built in
total, the last one in 1999, although in theory you could still buy one after
this. Only two of this total were VHPD engined, the rest being 1.6 and 1.8-
litre units (including VVC powerplants). As stated, the 21's main problem
was the iconic Lotus Elise, which offered a broader range of abilities for the
same sort of price. The 21 also offered less performance than a 7 for more
money, although it did counter with a very attractive, Lotus-inspired shape
and a smidgen more practicality.

138

The 21 did not die there, however, for there was a very exciting race car project, the 21 GTO. This was a fixed-roof 21 racer that evolved from the 1999 Belcar Belgian GT race winner. Its shape was derived from wind tunnel testing, producing an elegant coupé roofline and a front spoiler, tested at 56kg downforce at 100mph.

Its engine was the 230bhp R500 1.8-litre K-series unit and performance was not surprisingly very strong: during testing at the Milbrook proving ground, it recorded a maximum speed of 153mph and a 0–60mph time of 3.8 seconds and a 0–100mph time of 9.5 seconds. Inside the car was Stack racing instrumentation and a six-point roll-cage.

Caterham said at the time: 'This exciting road car is aimed at GT racing's under-2.0-litre class and serious track day customers.' At launch in October 2000, it even quoted a road or race spec price of £39,950.

Despite the fact that only the prototype had been built, the 21 GTO was still a live project at the time of writing, although where it would fit into the racing categories available is dubious. There is a GTO racing category in the UK for sub-2.0-litre (under 700kg) or over 2.0 litres (up to 1,100kg), at which level it would have to compete with the mighty Porsche 911 GT3. The 21 GTO was, however, quicker than the 7 Superlight racer, a remarkable fact considering it weighed one third more (the extra performance was gained from the wind tunnel-honed aerodynamics). Some non-GTO 21s did go racing, and a notable success was a class win at the 2000 Zolder 24-hour race, where it reliably out-performed race Elises.

Most 21s were fitted with 1.6 or 1.8-litre K-series engines, providing excellent acceleration and, thanks to far better aerodynamics, a much higher top speed than the 7.

This is the Belgian race-winning coupé that spawned the 21 GTO, a serious racer that was still a 'live' project in 2002.

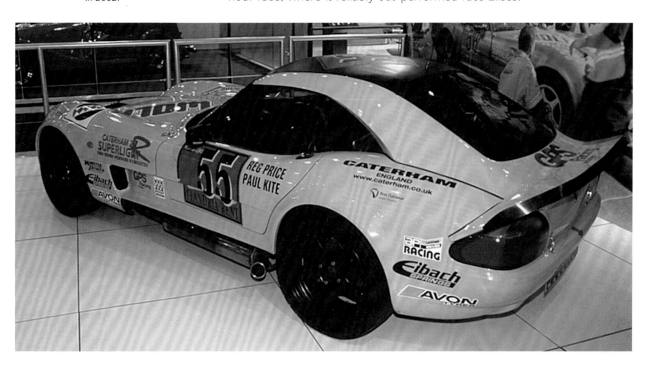

Approved modifications

Caterham now has a dedicated aftersales department specialising in maintaining, upgrading and personalising customer cars, for whatever purpose.

Upgrading a 7 is a very natural course to follow. Once you have got used to the performance and road potential of a 7, it is understandable if you want to extend the abilities of your car.

But which modifications are best? In order not to upset the balance of your 7 – which is the main reason for owning one, after all – your best course of action is to approach Caterham Cars. Approved modifications are always best for a number of reasons. First, every component has been either tested for its suitability in the 7, or engineered rigorously so that it works in the 7. Second, you will be getting a guarantee of the best level of service and the patina of factory approval.

Very much supporting this avenue, a new factory service is Caterham Aftersales, set up for maintaining, upgrading and personalising your 7. It advises on what upgrade or modification is best for you, your car and your wallet. Essentially it provides ways to upgrade your existing car, offering retro-fits that take advantage of recent improvements. Not only older models but more recent Classics and Roadsports can also be upgraded with handling, performance and cosmetic features.

Caterham Cars now has a CD-ROM of official parts and upgrades available, as well as a special area on their website detailing the various options.

Engine

Dry sump lubrication. This is currently standard on the R500 and Superlight R race car, and optional on all other models except the Classic. It can be fitted on any Rover (right-hand drive only), Ford crossflow or Vauxhall engine, with separate kits offered for each type.

Anti-cavitation oil tank. Caterham supplies an alloy tank and all necessary piping, providing most of the lubrication protection of a dry sump at a fraction of the cost.

Ultra-light competition flywheel. Available for Rover engines, this results in much greater responsiveness. There are in fact two versions: a lightweight one developed for the VHPD engine (Superlight R road car) and an ultra-light one for the R500.

Aluminium radiator. Lightweight radiators are available in either road or race forms, the ultimate version having a triple pass design to maximise cooling performance.

Integral restraint uprated engine mounting rubbers. These answer the criticism that previous versions allowed the rubbers to tear apart in an accident. The metal inserts in this interchangeable redesign prevent this.

Silicone cooling hose set. Available in various colours for Rover engines only.

Transmission

Six-speed gearbox. Caterham's in-house aluminium-cased close-ratio six-speed gearbox is widely acclaimed for its well-chosen ratios, ideally suited to the modern engines fitted to recent 7s, especially those that thrive on high revs rather than low-down torque. It is ultra-reliable and race proven and has been mandatory on Superlight and Roadsports models since 1998. A six-speed 'box is expensive to buy on its own (although Caterham will exchange one for your five-speed box at reduced cost), and will reward you with sweetly matched ratios, perfect for each up-change.

Competition clutch plate and cover. Plates and covers are available for Ford or Rover engines (the Rover versions developed by AP Racing).

Brakes

Aluminium brake master cylinder. Lightweight and reduces 'dead' pedal travel and operational travel, and increases pedal effort.

AP Racing/Caterham front discs with four-pot callipers. This 10-inch ventilated brake set-up is widely acclaimed and produces among the very best braking performance of any road car today. It is also lighter than the standard 9-inch disc and cast iron calliper set-up. It is possible to buy a complete uprated front brake kit.

Lightweight alloy front hub. This reduces weight on live axle equipped cars.

Suspension

Wide-track front suspension kit. Developed for the Superlight to provide an equal track front and rear, the wide-track front end provides extra grip and poise. Often referred to as Supersports suspension, it is standard on Superlight and Blackbird 7s, and on the wider SV model, and can be ordered for the Roadsport.

R500 aerofoil wishbones. The very elegant aerofoil-profile front wishbones fitted on the R500 can be ordered for other 7s at extra cost, as long as they are fitted with wide-track front suspension. They may have some aerodynamic advantage.

Damper ride height adjuster kit. This adjustable ride height set-up is available only for cars fitted with Bilstein dampers. Adjustable spring seats are also available.

Live axle Bilstein damper conversion kit. Bilstein dampers can be fitted to live axle Caterhams using this kit.

Wheels and tyres

Wheels
A very wide variety of wheels is suitable for fitting to the 7, but Caterham itself supplies the following:
- 13in alloys (6 x 13 Minator in silver or black, de Dion only; or 7 x 13 Minator)
- 13in magnesium alloys (R500 type magnesium split rim, 6.5 x 13 front, 8.5 x 13 rear, de Dion only)
- 14in alloys
- 15in alloys (Prisoner type)
- 16in five-spoke alloys

Locking wheel nut sets are also available.

Tyres
Caterham officially supplies:
- 13in Avon Road tyres (standard for Classic and Superlight).
- 13in Yokohama Sport A021R and A032R tyres (only available when adjustable spring seats are ordered) – no-cost option for Superlight, optional on Classic and Roadsport.
- 13in Avon Sport tyres (only available when adjustable spring seats are ordered) – standard on Blackbird and Superlight, optional for Roadsport; standard on 13in Mag alloys for R500.
- 14in Avon Road tyres (standard on Roadsport, no-cost option for Blackbird).
- 15in Avon Road tyres (optional for Roadsport only).
- 16in Avon Road tyres (optional for Roadsport only).

Bodywork

Carbon fibre bodywork. More interest is generated by carbon fibre body panels than any other body modification. This is because carbon fibre is very lightweight, very strong and has a certain patina of superiority. Requests for carbon fibre panels have grown massively at Caterham since the success of the Superlight models to which they are fitted.

A carbon fibre package of nose cone and wings is a £1,200 option on all new Caterhams except the Superlight models where it is standard. Front wings can be ordered to fit either 13–14in wheels or 15–16in wheels.

Other popular carbon fibre items are lightweight rear wing protectors, rear-view mirrors (both centre and side mirrors available), front indicator cones and sill protectors for the step-over body sides. Interior carbon fibre items are treated separately below.

Black pack. This black package is for the windscreen frame and stanchions, exhaust guard and headlight bowls. It is fitted as standard to the Superlight and Blackbird, but is optional for other models.

Full windscreen and wipers. Of current Caterham models, a windscreen is only actually standard for the Roadsport model, and optional on all others. If you plan to use your 7 for anything other than very occasional blasts or track days, a windscreen becomes virtually essential – despite the fact that it adds weight and turbulence. Having either 'Brooklands' aero screens (as on the Classic) or a full-width aero screen (as on the Superlight) renders you open to tremendous wind flow, the full force of the elements and stray flying stones. Ideally you should be wearing a helmet or at least goggles and a hat to avoid the potential debris if you do not fit a full screen. Caterham's windscreen has a heated element in it that solves all demisting problems.

Full-width aero screens. The full-width aero screen is a popular item if you want to duplicate the Superlight look in a lesser 7. Two types are available: the carbon fibre screen as fitted to the R500, or the black composite screen as fitted to the Superlight.

Wind deflector kit. This adds transparent wind deflectors to the windscreen pillars, deflecting wind away from the cockpit when you are travelling without side screens at modest speeds.

Carbon fibre body items are among the most popular retro-fit items. As well as the nose cone pictured, you can get carbon fibre wings, wing protectors, aero screen, mirrors and interior parts.

The 'black pack' consists of changing the chrome parts – windscreen, headlamps and exhaust guard – to black.

Weather equipment. This is still only standard on the Roadsport, and optional on all other models. The full soft-top, hood sticks and side screen package requires that you have a windscreen fitted. The current design is far better than the pre-1988 fixed side screen type, having better elbow room and folding side screens that can be placed in the boot. The actual hood itself is fiddly to erect and stretches and contracts according to weather conditions. It also makes the cockpit resonate to a far greater degree, increasing interior sound levels. But at least it provides some basic protection from the rain.

Also available is a hood bag to store the roof, a tonneau cover to keep the cockpit covered, or alternatively a tonneau cover with half sidescreens. Full car covers are also available for indoor and outdoor applications.

Rear luggage rack. Having a limited boot area is a limitation to overall practicality, so Caterham markets a luggage rack that mounts behind the spare wheel. It incorporates luggage straps.

Roll bars. FIA approved roll bars are available for competition use only in de Dion or live axle long cockpit types. A popular extra for road cars is the lightweight R500 roll bar. Having been developed for the R500 (and fitted only on the R500 and Blackbird), it became standard for all de Dion-equipped cars from 2001.

Fuel filler flap. For external fuel filler 7s, a popular option is Caterham's aluminium flush-fitting fuel filler flap, which is fully lockable.

Interior

Carbon fibre dashboard. Standard on Blackbird and Superlight models, the evocative carbon fibre dashboard is a £150 option for other models.

Seats. Which seats to fit to your 7 is a difficult choice. While earlier cars had a fixed bench, the advent of individual seats opens up a variety of possibilities. Caterham currently offers options of upholstery in cloth or leather, plus the options of composite race seats (standard on the Superlight and Blackbird, a no-cost option on the Classic and Roadsport), or Kevlar race seats (standard on the R500, optional on others).

S-Type trim. Oxted Trimming supplies the S-Type trim package in either half-leather or full-leather types. The leather trim route has dramatically dropped off in popularity such that they are now available to special order only.

Steering wheel. The standard choice for the base 7 until September 2001 was a Mountney steering wheel, but this has now upgraded to a Motolita leather steering wheel (previously optional for the Classic and Roadsport models). Options include a Momo leather steering wheel (standard on Superlight models and the Blackbird) and a quick-release kit (only for the Momo wheel), which is standard on the Superlight and R500, and optional for other models. The latter is an excellent security device and helps you feel like a racing driver!

An aluminium flush-fitting fuel filler cap looks good and is secure against tampering.

144

Aluminium handbrake sleeve. This elegant metal handbrake lever cover is suitable for post-1996 central handbrakes only (and standard on the R500).

Aluminium gear knob. The aluminium knob can be ordered with 5 or 6-speed gate patterns marked on it.

Heater. The advent of the Classic and Superlight models relegated the heater to become standard only for the Roadsport. If you want to keep warm at the expense of adding weight to your 7, one can be ordered as an optional extra on any car.

Roll cages are wise fitments if you are serious about track days. This roadgoing R500 has a Superlight R racer full FIA roll cage fitted.

Floor coverings. Both a rubber floormat set and a tailored carpet set are available from Caterham.

Audio systems. This may seem delightfully irrelevant in the 7, but Caterham offers an Alpine hi-fi system as an option (as fitted to the *Autosport* edition). The author has a colleague who has a 7 fitted with a CD autochanger in the boot . . .

Harnesses. A competition-inspired restraint system that looks great and provides extra safety on road cars is a four-point harness. These are available from Caterham in red, blue or black (and come as standard on Superlight models and the Blackbird). Arm restraints and a crutch strap are additional extras for four-point harnesses, converting them into six-point harnesses.

Security

Immobiliser. Caterham began fitting Vecta immobilisers in the 1990s, but built-in engine immobilisers are now standard across the range (except the Classic and R500, which can be so fitted at extra cost).

Battery master switch kit. For use in competitive motorsport.

Fire extinguisher. Required for competition.

Competition parts

Caterham offers a huge selection of competition parts, including various items of safety equipment, carbon fibre body panels (which are not however allowed in Caterham's own race series), uprated brakes (for Superlight R racers only) and uprated suspension.

Four-point harnesses in various colours keep you strapped safely in place.

Caterham Race Cars

Racing and 7s go hand-in-hand. The car that was branded 'too fast to race' in America is an ideal tool in which to compete, whether in sprints, hill-climbs or circuit events. Several thousand 7s are reckoned to be racing worldwide.

Indeed, one of the main reasons why people buy a 7 is that they are thinking of using it in some form of competitive motorsport. Straight out of the box, it can be competitive in a huge variety of racing events.

The highest profile racing is undoubtedly the four official race series run by Caterham. Dozens of cars sold by Caterham each year are destined for the factory-sponsored race series, which have been running since 1986 and have proven immensely popular.

Historically there have been three series running concurrently since the outset (upped to four since 1997 and expanding all the time). At the bottom rung was an entry-level class for less powerful cars, the middle rung was for more highly tuned and modified cars, while the top class always represented the most powerful Caterham models.

Initially all three series were for roadgoing cars, going back to the grass-roots days of 7 motorsports when owners would drive to circuits, race and then drive home again in the same car. From 1991, the most senior class – the Vauxhall Challenge – abandoned the rule that cars should be road-legal

146

(although they could be converted to road use because the chassis was essentially the same). The category switched to Rover K-series Superlight in time, still with slick tyres and circuit specification.

For 1995, a new entry-level series was created called the Scholarship (later renamed the Academy). This was for absolute novices and represented superb value and an ideal gateway into competitive motorsport. Initially the racer was based on the Ford 100bhp Sprint engine with a reconditioned live axle and five-speed Ford V6 gearbox. For 1997 it switched to Vauxhall 1.6 power and later to 1.6 K-series. Many of the Scholarship/Academy cars found their way back on to the road as non-racers and should be no different to any equivalent 7 model.

Action from the Superlight R series, which provides some of the most competitive and enjoyable motorsport in the world.

Currently there are four officially supported Caterham race series, providing a full spread of racing for all levels. The entry level is the incredibly popular Academy which introduces total novices to the sport. This category's popularity is no surprise; an all-inclusive subsidised price (£14,950 for 2002) offers a complete package – sponsored car, entry fees, club membership, racing medical, test day with instruction and full tuition for a National 'B' licence. The competitor's hand is held throughout the season's racing, which is important because the requirement for entry is that the driver should never have held a racing licence before. It is not only circuit races but speed events, hill-climbs, sprints and a kart race. A maximum of 50 competitors may take part each year.

Having run on Vauxhall power, for the 2001 season the Academy switched to 115bhp 1.6 K-series engines because the rear axle could cope with more power. The specification is strictly set and cannot be deviated from. Also with the K-series engine, if you wanted to upgrade to senior categories using the same car, you could do so (unlike the old Vauxhall racers).

This is salient because, once you have raced in the Academy one season, you must move on. The natural progression is the Graduate series, founded in 1997 and open to ex-Academy and any other competition licence-holding drivers alike. The vehicle specification follows the Academy racer exactly, and all cars must be genuine ex-Championship cars or new Academy cars from the factory. The emphasis is on fun rather than high-cost campaigning, and this is another very popular series. There is also now a Super Graduate series with the 1.8-litre 138bhp engine and Avon slick tyres.

One step up again is the Roadsport Championship. Launched in 1998, it is based around a 133bhp 1.6 K-series Supersport engined, six-speed 7 in Roadsport guise (i.e. road legal with a windscreen, lighting and so on). A fast and competitive formula, it attracts entries from a wide variety of racers and concentrates on circuit racing, maximising track time.

The most senior Caterham race category is the Superlight Challenge. The 1.8 K-series VHPD dry-sump powerplant develops 200bhp in race trim. With their full FIA roll cages, Avon slick tyres, stripped-out lightweight

specification and ferocious pace, they look and perform on another level entirely. This is racing for experienced drivers, highly competitive, and often backed by professional teams.

The newest championship is the Euro Cup, a series for Superlight racers (with Yokohama slick tyres). It features five rounds at legendary European circuits: Nürburgring, Spa, Zandvoort, Dijon and Brands Hatch.

Of course, there is plenty of racing opportunity outside the main Caterham championships. Notably, the 750 Motorclub runs its own championships for the 7, including six and 12-hour relay races. There are numerous other categories in which the 7 is eligible to race.

Sprinting and hill-climbing remain the easiest and cheapest ways to drive competitively. These 'speed events' pit you against the clock as you try to complete a circuit or a hill route in the fastest possible time. Sevens are extremely competitive in such disciplines and can nearly always be seen in action at speed events. Various categories are open to 7s. The Caterham Motorsports Club (see below) also organises competitive events, such as Slalom (a timed challenge run at Brooklands using identical 7s).

Caterham Motorsports Club

This club was set up by Caterham to bring 'a taste of motorsport to enthusiasts everywhere'. It is intended both as a gateway to extend your abilities as a driver in your own 7 and to sample the potential of the car even if you are not a 7 owner.

Several events are organised. The Circuit Experience is an opportunity to drive a 7 with a qualified race instructor to give tuition on track. The day includes a briefing, demonstration drive, tuition, fast-lap ride in the 200bhp Superlight racer, helmet hire, refreshments and track time.

If you own a 7 and want to take it on the track, the Motorsports Club organises owners' days at famous UK circuits. The format is similar to the Circuit Experience, except you drive your own car in group sessions organised according to previous experience. Of course, there are dozens of other track day organisations and events on tracks around the country, at which 7s are the staple raw material and frequently the quickest cars around.

Buying an ex-race car

Ex-racers make ideal choices for the driver who plans to use the 7 primarily for track days, sprints and hill-climbs. They are ideally set up for competitive use and also tend to be a little cheaper than their road-going equivalents.

You might also consider going racing yourself, but if you are interested in the official race series you will need to contact Caterham to check about eligibility. Normally the rules mean that you'll have to buy your car new from Caterham but in certain cases – such as the Graduate series – a car from the previous season can be raced without a problem.

Virtually all racers will have had some sort of shunt in their career. However, major repairs are quite feasible with the 7 and it's really the quality of the fix that you should be concentrating on. Follow the general advice given in the chapter on Buying, Running and Restoring a 7 – but even more strictly – and you won't go far wrong, but as a rule of thumb those racers that were run by teams will usually have been treated better than those run by individuals.

Many racers have an established provenance and it's worth getting in touch with the person who raced the car to find out a bit of its history. Was it a race winner? Was it run by a team or an individual? What was its accident record?

Converting a race car for road use

The beauty of the Caterham is that racing machines are very close to their roadgoing equivalents, and vice versa. The 7 is as close to a road racer as you are going to get, as proven by the fact that the rules in some categories of Caterham racing require that the cars are road-registered and road-legal.

Many ex-racers make their way on to the road once they are retired. Converting one can be as simple as removing the racing numbers: it's as simple as that! However, if you're going to use the car on the road, you will probably want a passenger seat and some interior trim, you may want to remove the battery cut-off switch and you might not necessarily want a fire extinguisher cluttering up the cabin. And having a full race roll cage may not be ideal for road use – although if you are doing a lot of track days, the added protection of a roll cage adds a lot of confidence.

In the case of dedicated racers such as the Vauxhall or Superlight series, these are not required to be road legal. Here, if you're buying a car straight off the grid there will be much more work to do: fitting lights, trim, road tyres and dashboard instrumentation for example.

One advantage of ex-race cars is that often they have a higher specification than road cars. For example, the 2001 Academy racer has 13-inch wheels with Avon CR322 185-section tyres (although it lacks a passenger seat and interior trim). Likewise the 2001 Superlight Challenge racer gearbox has stronger cross-gate springing for fast circuit work, but it retains the old-type transmission tunnel without the handbrake.

Modifying a car for race use

If you want to race in one of the popular and highly competitive Caterham race series, you must abide by the strict regulations governing each category. This will usually mean the purchase of a brand new car from the factory (the Graduate series however allows for ex-Championship cars to be raced). Caterham Cars will guide you.

Other racing categories have their own rulebooks, which must always be strictly adhered to. Safety is always the number one priority, so be sure your roll cage, fire extinguisher, battery cut-off and safety harnesses are professionally fitted according to the various formulae. Always fully apprise yourself of the regulations and customs of the racing body to which you will belong.

Many of the cars from the old Vauxhall race series (seen here in action in 1994) find their way back on to the road. Check for chassis damage.

Safety items are essential to go racing. Helmets, fire extinguishers, roll-over protection and (pictured here) a battery cut-off switch are vital.

Production evolution
7 chronology

The 7 legend started as early as 1957 with the launch of the Series 1.

1957 Lotus Mk 7 launched at London Motor Show with Ford 100E sidevalve engine. Prototype's de Dion rear axle and disc brakes changed for Austin Metropolitan axle and drum brakes on production cars.

1958 Coventry Climax FWA 1100 engine and BMC four-speed gearbox fitted to new 'Super 7' model. Worm and nut steering changed to modified Morris 1000 rack and pinion.

1959 Lotus 7A launched using BMC A-series engine and gearbox from Austin A35. Other models redesignated 7F (Ford) and 7C (Coventry Climax). Steering changed to Triumph Herald rack-and-pinion in October.

1960 7 America launched in January with Sprite engine, 'clamshell' flared glassfibre wings and tubular bumpers. Original Rubery Owen wheels changed to Triumph TR3. Series 2 launched in June with simplified chassis, Triumph Herald front uprights, 13-inch wheels in place of 15-inch, rear suspension A-frame, Standard Companion rear axle, relocated steering rack, restyled nose (now glassfibre not aluminium), reprofiled rear wings, red-trimmed interior.

The Series 2 evolved with more power and a simpler chassis.

1961 Ford 105E engine fitted for the first time from January, within 1–2 years replacing both the 100E and BMC A-series powered cars. Mid-year, the new Super 7 was launched with a Cosworth-modified 1,340cc Ford engine (SCCA versions available for USA).

1962 Super 7 1500 launched in September with Ford Cortina 1.5-litre engine. Cosworth tuned versions also available. Fuel tank expanded from 5.5 gallons to 8 gallons.

1963 Cycle wings replaced by standard flared wings.

1967 'Series 2½' introduced, with Ford 1600 crossflow engine.

1968 Launch of Series 3 in September with 1300 or 1600 Ford crossflow engines, Ford Escort Mexico rear axle, wider rear wings, new front hubs, Lotus Cortina or Brand Lotus wheels, standard front disc brakes, Ford Escort rear drums, revised instrumentation, negative earth electrics.

1969 1600 Holbay-powered 7S displayed in January but never enters production. Instead, Lotus Twin Cam powered SS becomes the ultimate Series 3 model, launched in October.

The Lotus Twin Cam engine was the mainstay of the 7 through the 1970s.

1970 Series 4 introduced with all-new glassfibre body, new space frame chassis with folded steel crossmember, rear axle located by Watts linkages and triangulated arm, double wishbone suspension from Lotus Europa, Burman rack-and-pinion steering, 1600 crossflow or Lotus Twin Cam engine.

1972 Production of Lotus 7 S4 believed to have ceased.

1973 S4 production restarts at Caterham with no modifications other than badging.

1974 Caterham 7 S4 replaced by revised Series 3 with Lotus Big Valve Twin Cam engine and strengthened Lotus S3 chassis.

Series 3 fixed the 'classic' 7 look and Ford crossflow/Lotus Twin Cam power options.

1975 Entry-level 7 reinstated with crossflow engines from Ford (1300 offered for one year only, 1600 also available from 1975 becomes the standard choice). Rear axle switched from Mk 1 Ford Escort to Mk 1 Escort RS, then Mk 2.

1976 Improved seating, KN 6J alloy wheel option.

1978 Ford Escort Mk 2 RS rear axle becomes standard.

1980 Caterham develops 1600 Sprint engine (uprated Ford Kent unit with 110bhp). Morris Ital rear axle launched to replace old Escort Mk 2 axle (production-ready from 1981). Ford Escort Sport gearbox replaces previous Ford 2000E 'box. Revised wiring loom and rocker switches fitted.

1981 Silver Jubilee model first seen (in production until 1983). Vegantune VTA twin-cam engine first fitted.

1982 Suspension spring rates increased and front brake pad material upgraded. Long cockpit chassis offered as an option.

1984 Cosworth 1600 BDR engine (150bhp) introduced in the 7. Caterham-modified 1700 Supersprint engine (135bhp) introduced. Lightweight radiator installed. Triumph Spitfire steering rack replaced by modified Mini rack. 7 relaunched in basic kit form as well as component form.

1985 Caterham-designed de Dion rear end offered as an option.

1986 Five-speed Ford Sierra V6 (XR4i) gearbox first offered in de Dion axle cars. 170bhp Cosworth BDR engine now available; this engine fitted with rear anti-roll bar, limited slip differential and individually adjustable seats is called the HPC. Symmetrical 'universal' chassis introduced with front cruciform and additional upper engine bay diagonal. VDO instruments and new wiring loom. Radiator upgraded and mounted on front of chassis.

1987 Chassis upgraded with powder coating for corrosion protection. Heated windscreen introduced.

1988 Disc brakes now fitted all round on de Dion-equipped cars, revised suspension settings (camber, toe-in, bump steer, spring rates all modified). Pedal box replaces original bracket. Practicality enhanced by larger, folding sidescreens with increased visibility and extra elbow room.

1989 Prisoner special edition launched with special paint scheme and dash plaque. 15-inch 'Prisoner' wheels and tyres introduced for better ride, grip and stability. Ignition timing modified to allow use of unleaded fuel in Ford engines. Aluminium fuel tank introduced. Chassis tubes made smaller.

1990 Vauxhall 2.0-litre HPC engine option launched with 175bhp (in production from 1991). Honeycomb side impact protection fitted to all chassis. Improved front suspension location with front half link added to top wishbone. Inertia reel seat belts introduced.

1991 Launch of Rover K-series powered 7 (in production from 1992). Bilstein suspension introduced with adjustable front geometry; revised dampers, spring rates, anti-roll bars.

1992 Low-cost GTS model first produced but only for a few months, as the even more stripped-out Classic takes over the entry-level reins. Specially painted 35th Anniversary model launched. Ultra-high performance JPE launched with lightweight carbon fibre panels, 250bhp SRE-tuned Vauxhall 2.0-litre engine, Quaife gearbox, special dash and seats.

1993 7 passes Low Volume Type Approval, allowing it to be sold fully-built for the first time ever (K-series and Vauxhall HPC engines only). Public launch of new Caterham-developed six-speed gearbox. Introduction of tuned K-series Supersport engine (128bhp). New grille with '7' logo launched for HPC. Swiss Caterham distributor launches S7 Competition R with 300bhp turbocharged Opel 2.0-litre engine.

With the de Dion rear axle, Caterham advanced the handling and ride significantly.

1994 Enlarged foot box gives extra leg room. Common chassis now fitted for Rover, Ford and Vauxhall engines. Public launch of Caterham 21 at Birmingham Motor Show.

1995 Six-speed gearbox enters production.

1996 1.6-litre K-series and 1.6-litre Supersport replace 1.4-litre (Road-Sport limited edition marks end of 1.4-litre engine). Revised stiffened chassis, revised suspension, new seats, handbrake resited to centre tunnel, Caterham-branded instruments and new lightweight loom. 40th Anniversary

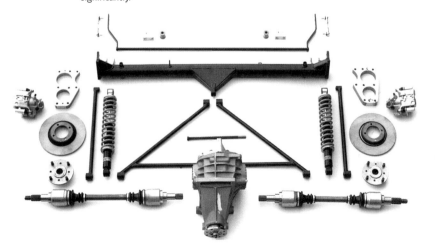

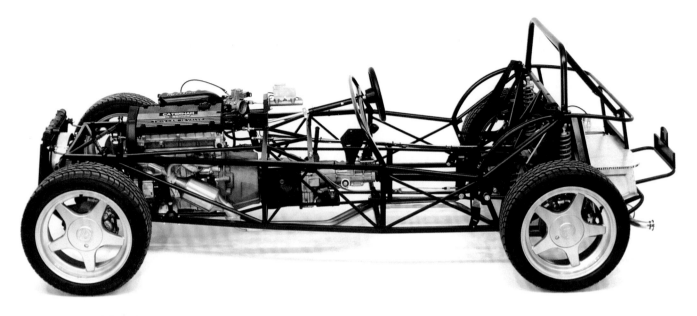

Rover K-series power introduced a new light alloy twin-cam engine family in 1991.

Caterham's own six-speed gearbox, launched in 1995, offers perfect ratios for the 7.

special edition launched. Ultra-light K-series 1.6-litre engined Superlight launched. Caterham 21 enters production.

1997 Superlight R version launched with tuned VHPD K-series engine (190bhp). Classic model gets Vauxhall 1600 engine. 1.8-litre K-series engine now available in standard and Supersport forms.

1998 VVC-powered 1.8-litre 7 launched. Aluminium Silverstone displayed, forms basis of Japanese limited edition car. Classic Supersprint launched with enlarged (1.8-litre) Vauxhall engine. ClubSport launched as track day orientated car, but is short-lived.

1999 Superlight R500 launched with very special 230bhp tuned K-series engine and 500bhp per tonne. Standard K-series 7 range renamed Roadsport. Ford Zetec-powered 7 launched in America. Final 21 built, although it continues in price lists.

A new interior for 1996 featured revised instrumentation.

2000 Caterham productionises a 7 with Honda Blackbird superbike engine and sequential gearbox. SV arrives as the first ever 7 that significantly alters the external shape of the original 7: it is wider and longer to release extra cockpit room. Autosport 50th Anniversary special edition launched.

2001 First major chassis overhaul since 1996 – the so-called '2001½' – incorporates some of the features of the R500 lightweight chassis. Honda FireBlade engine available through James Whiting. Beaulieu edition launched as better-equipped Classic. Mountney steering wheel deleted and Motolita leather item made standard on Classic and Roadsport.

Major engineering developments

Engines

1957-62	Ford 100E sidevalve; 1,172cc; 30-48bhp
1958-60	Coventry Climax FWA 1100; 1,098cc; 75bhp
1959-61	BMC A-series (Austin A35/Morris Minor, Austin-Healey Sprite for USA); 948cc; 37-43bhp
1960-61	Austin-Healey Sprite for USA; 1,098cc; 55bhp
1961-68	Ford Anglia 105E; 997cc; 39bhp
1961-62	Ford 109E Classic Cosworth; 1,340cc; 85bhp
1962-68	Ford 116E Cortina 1500GT; 1,498cc; 66bhp (Cosworth version 95bhp)
1968-73/ 1975-76	Ford 225E Cortina 1300; 1,297cc; 72bhp
1968-98	Ford 225E Cortina 1600GT; 1,598cc; 84bhp
1969	Holbay-tuned Cortina 1600; 1,598cc; 120bhp
1969-73	Lotus Twin Cam (Special Equipment or Holbay Big Valve versions); 1,558cc; 115-125bhp
1973-78	Lotus Big Valve Twin Cam (latterly assembled by Vegantune); 1,558cc; 126bhp
1978-83	Lotus/Vegantune Tall Block Twin Cam; 1,598cc; 126bhp
1980-98	Caterham Sprint (modified Ford 1600 crossflow); 1,598cc; 100-110bhp
1981-85	Vegantune VTA Twin Cam; 1,598cc; 130bhp
1982-84	Holbay 1700; 1,699cc; 140bhp
1983-96	Cosworth BDR 1600; 1,599cc; 150bhp (claimed) 140bhp (actual)
1984-98	Caterham Supersprint (modified Ford 1600 crossflow); 1,691cc; 135bhp
1985-95	Cosworth BDR 1700; 1,699cc; 170bhp (claimed) 160bhp (actual)

1986-91	Ford XR3i CVH (optional turbocharging); 1,596cc; 105-132bhp
1990-98	Caterham-Vauxhall Astra GTE; 1,998cc; 165-175bhp (Evolution 218-235bhp)
1991-96	Caterham-Rover K-series 1.4; 1,397cc; 103-110bhp
1992-2001	Caterham-Vauxhall JPE; 1,998cc; 250bhp
1995-2001	Opel Rallye Turbo; 1,998cc; 300bhp
1993-97	Caterham-Rover K-series 1.4 Supersport; 1,397cc; 128bhp
1996-date	Caterham-Rover K-series 1.6/1.6 Supersport; 1,588cc; 115-138bhp
1997-date	Caterham-Rover K-series 1.8/1.8 Supersport; 1,796cc; 122-140bhp
1997-date	Caterham-Rover VHPD (Very High Performance Derivative); 1,796cc; 190bhp (200bhp racer)
1998-date	Caterham-Rover K-series 1.8 VVC; 1,796cc; 150bhp
1998-99	Caterham Supersprint (modified); 1,760cc; 146bhp
1998-date	Caterham-Vauxhall Supersprint; 1,796cc; 120bhp
1999-date	Caterham-Rover K-series 1.8 Superlight R500; 1,796cc;230bhp
1999-date	Ford Zetec USA; 1,988cc; 135bhp
2000-2001	Honda Blackbird; 1,137cc; 170bhp
2001-date	Honda FireBlade; 919cc/929cc; 125-150bhp

Gearboxes

1957-62	Ford 100E 3-speed
1958-61	BMC Austin A30/Sprite four-speed
1961-68	Ford Anglia 105E four-speed
1961-62	Ford 109E Classic four-speed
1962-68	Ford 116E Cortina four-speed
1968-69	Ford 225E Cortina four-speed

1970-81	Ford 2821E Corsair four-speed
1981-98	Ford Escort Sport four-speed
1986-date	Ford Sierra V6 XR4i five-speed
1992-99	Quaife straight-cut five-speed (JPE)
1993-date	Caterham six-speed
2000-2001	Honda Blackbird six-speed sequential
2001-date	Honda FireBlade six-speed sequential

Suspension

1957-60	Independent front suspension by transverse wishbones incorporating anti-roll bar. Rear live axle located by twin trailing radius arms and diagonal link. Coil spring/damper units all round.
1960-69/ 1974-80	As above, but Triumph Herald (later Spitfire Mk IV) front uprights, rear axle suspended by under-slung A-frame and twin trailing links.
1980-98	As above, but adjustable Spax dampers.
1998-date	As above, but Bilstein dampers.
1985-91	Caterham de Dion rear suspension option with Spax dampers.
1990-2000	Half-link on top front wishbone (live axle cars).
1991-date	Bilstein suspension with adjustable rear anti-roll bar.
1996-date	Revised front and rear suspension geometry. Wide-track front suspension option (standard on Superlight models).
2001-date	Revised suspension geometry.

Rear axles and brakes

| 1957-60 | Live rear axle from Austin/Nash Metropolitan. 8in drum brakes front and rear (BMC initially, later Triumph Herald). |
| 1960-68 | Standard Companion live rear axle with 8in front and 7in rear drum brakes. |

1962-68   (Super 7 1500) As above but Girling 9½in front disc brakes.

1968-69/   As 1960-68, but Girling (Triumph Spitfire) 9in disc brakes
1974-77   and 7in rear drums.

1977-80   As above but with Ford RS, then RS2000, rear axle. 9in
                Escort RS rear drums, dual circuit brakes from 1978.

1980-date As above but Morris Marina/Ital live rear axle, Marina 8in rear
                drum brakes, adjustable Spax dampers.

1985-88   De Dion rear axle option based around Ford Sierra
                differential, with Ford Sierra 9in rear drum brakes.

1988-date As above but rear end has 9in disc brakes.

1996-date Optional 10-inch ventilated front discs and four-pot callipers
                (standard on Superlight models).

Useful contacts

Caterham Cars must be your first port of call for spare parts, factory upgrades and modifications. The factory now operates a dedicated aftersales department.

Companies

Caterham Cars Ltd (showroom
    and sales)
Station Avenue,
Caterham,
Surrey CR3 6LB
Tel: 07000 000077
www.caterham.co.uk

Caterham Cars Ltd (factory)
2 Kennet Road,
Dartford,
Kent DA1 4QN
Tel: 01322 625800 (switchboard)
    01322 625804 (aftersales)

Arch Motor & Manufacturing
    Co. Ltd
Redwongs Way, Huntingdon,
Cambs PE29 7HD
Tel: 01480 459661
Official chassis supplier

Oxted Trimming Co. Ltd
14a Beatrice Road,
Oxted,
Surrey RH8 0PZ
Tel: 01883 712112
Official trim supplier

Approved Caterham Cars service and sales centres

East Anglia
Hyperion Motorsport,
3 Sudbury Road, Little Maplestead,
    Essex
Tel: 01787 478800
*Official Caterham Motorsport
    Centre*

London
Ratrace Motorsport,
9b Atlas Trading Estate,
Oxgate Lane, London
Tel: 020 8830 5677)

Midlands
Caterham Midlands, The Knoll,
Leicester Road, Leicester
Tel: 01455 841616

Sebah Automotive, Nottingham
Tel: 01636 813493

North East
Auto Centre,
198 Neasham Road,
Darlington, Co Durham
Tel: 01325 480035

North West
John Noble Motorsport,
Chatsworth Business Park,
Chesterfield
Tel: 01246 483867

Ryders of Liverpool,
113 Liverpool Road, Crosby,
Liverpool
Tel: 0151 922 7585

South East
Redline Components,
Caterham, Surrey
Tel: 01883 346515

Caterham Cars,
Caterham, Surrey
Tel: 01883 333700

Caterham Cars,
Dartford, Kent
Tel: 01322 625800

South West
Millwood Motor Co.,
Mill Garage, Cam,
Dursley, Gloucestershire
Tel: 01453 544321
www.millwood-mc.com

Midway Motors,
Yelland Road, Barnstaple, Devon
Tel: 01271 861083

Scotland
MB Jarvie
Tel: 0141 429 7339

Fairways, Kilbowie Road, Glasgow
Tel: 01389 878666

Wales
Kenrick Motors,
Llangollen
Tel; 01978 861382

Overseas agents: see website
http://www.caterham.co.uk for
full listing.

Motorsports

Caterham race co-ordinator:
Entreprix Ltd, Belinda Edwards
Tel: 01379 890703

*Caterham race sponsorship
consultant:*
Hyperion, Magnus Laird
Tel: 01787 478800

Racing clubs:
BRSCC, John Ward
Tel: 01732 848884
BRDC, Chris Norman
Tel: 01327 320287
BARC, Dennis Carter
Tel: 01264 772607
750 MC, Robin Knight
Tel: 01379 384268

Caterham Motorsports Club,
Paul Kite Tel: 01883 333700

**Selected independent 7
specialists**

James Whiting Sevens
Ashford, Middlesex
Tel: 01784 241466
www.jameswhiting.co.uk
*Very long-standing 7 specialist, and
official Fireblade agent.*

South West Lotus Centre
Lifton, Devon
Tel: 01566 784152
www.thelotuscentre.fsnet.co.uk

The 7 Workshop (and Roger King
engines)
Hoddesdon, Herts.
Tel: 01992 470480
http://freespace.virgin.net/seven.wo
rkshop

Woodcote Sports Cars
Merstham, Surrey
Tel: 01737 645213
www.racecar.co.uk/woodcote
Used Caterham 7 sales

Paul Matty Sports Cars
Bromsgrove, Worcestershire
Tel: 01527 835656
www.racecar.co.uk/pmattysportscars

Clubs

Lotus Seven Club
PO Box 7,
Cranleigh,
Surrey GU6 8YP
Tel/Fax: 01483 277172
www.lotus7club.co.uk

This is the only British club
dedicated to Lotus and Caterham
Sevens. It has a monthly magazine
(called *Low Flying*), which prints
news, views, technical discussions
and members' stories. The club
offers insurance discounts,
organises track days (with tuition
available), runs hill-climb and sprint
series, promotes regional groups,
sells regalia, offers technical help,
and organises an international
meeting in Britain plus an annual
trip to Le Mans. Other benefits
include factory visits, organised
driving 'marathons', and visits to
GP teams, shows and museums.
Membership is free with the
purchase of any new Caterham.

Insurance

Adrian Flux
Tel: 08700 777888
www.caterhaminsurance.co.uk

TC Lowes
Tel: 0207 220 7878
www.caterhamcarinsurance.co.uk

Competition Car Insurance
Tel: 0115 941 5255
www.competition-car-
insurance.co.uk
*Insurance for racing and track
days.*

Selected websites

Official
Caterham Cars (UK)
www.caterham.co.uk

USA
www.uscaterham.com

France
www.caterham-france.fr

Unofficial
www.lotus7register.co.uk
Part of the Lotus 7 Club site,
providing lots of data about the
history of the Lotus 7 specifically.

www.supersevenlinks.com
Wide variety of links to sites of
Lotus/Caterham 7 interest.

www.r500owners.com
Site for Superlight R500 owners

www.caterhamweb.co.uk
7s for sale, lots more about 7s